CULTURE SHOCK!

SUCCEED IN BUSINESS

The essential guide for business and investment

Philippines

Joaquin L. Gonzalez
& Luis R.Calingo

D0557940

Graphic Arts Center Publishing Company
Portland, Oregon

S

Photo credits:
Bong Cayabyab, 120, 138, 163
Joaquin L. Gonzalez, 15, 112, 146
Philippine Department of Tourism, 21, 43, 58, 66, 86, 150, 166
Map on p 37 taken from the book *The Pearl Road: Tales of Treasure Ships in the Philippines* by Christophe Loviny

© 1998 Times Editions Pte Ltd

This book is published by special
arrangement with Times Editions Pte Ltd
Times Centre, 1 New Industrial Road, Singapore 536196
International Standard Book Number 1-55868-413-1
Library of Congress Catalog Number 98-84832
Graphic Arts Center Publishing Company
P.O. Box 10306 • Portland, Oregon 97296-0306 • (503) 226-2402

Printed in Singapore

Contents

Acknowledgements   6

Introduction   8

Map of Philippines   10

Chapter 1 — Outlook for the Philippines   11
    Leaving Behind the Past 11
    Strengthening Bilateral, Regional and Global Ties 23
    Other Multilateral Linkages 34

Chapter 2 — Philippine History for the Business Person   36
    Precolonial Economic System 36
    Colonial Economy (1521–1946) 38
    World War II and Japan 43
    Post-Independence Administrations (1946–1964) 44
    Marcos and Martial Law (1965–1986) 46
    Redemocratisation and Market Liberalisation (1986–Present) 47

Chapter 3 — Government and Politics for the
                Business Person   53
    Philippine Government 53
    The Armed Forces of the Philippines 62
    Constitutions (1935, 1973 & 1987) 63
    Philippine Politics for the Business Person 64
    Political Parties and Interest Groups 68
    Church and Politics 69
    Electoral Contests 70

Chapter 4 — Getting Your Business Started   **72**

Organising the Business Enterprise 72

Forming a Philippine Corporation 76

Investment Procedures and Requirements 77

Exporting to the Philippines 82

Banking and Foreign Exchange 84

Taxation 92

Manpower and Labour Relations 93

Immigration and Customs 102

Environmental Regulations 105

Protection of Investments and Intellectual Property 107

Acquisition of Land 110

Chapter 5 — Present and Future Niches   **112**

Subic Bay Freeport and Clark Special Economic Zone 113

Public-Private Partnerships in Infrastructure and Utilities 120

Regional Public and Private Investment Centres
   for Agro-industrial and Manufacturing 124

Tourism Investments 137

Tourist Accommodation and Transportation Facilitites 144

Chapter 6 — Management Matters   **145**

Filipino Management Style 145

The Role of the Filipino Women in Business and Society 154

Chapter 7 — Culture, Customs and Communication   **156**

Filipino Cultural Values 156

Interpersonal Relations 158

Social Organisation 162

Poverty 165

Languages 168
Religious Life 170
Education 171
Body Language, Gestures and Greetings 174
Useful Phrases 175

Appendices

A Basic Facts and Travel Tips   177
B Directory of Important Contacts   185
C References   197

Notes   199

About the Authors   201

Index   202

Acknowledgements

Many individuals and organisations provided invaluable support to the research and writing of this book. We would like to express sincere appreciation to our family and friends. They include the Gonzalez, Calingo, Borbon, Bantug and Yulo families, Bong Bengzon, Marcelo Ang, Chil Soriano, Mila Bernardo, Marivic Sarmiento, Ed Campos, Jim Ellis, Prospy Hernandez, Patrick Chiong, Rollie Buendia, Ronnie Holmes, Wilfrido Villacorta, Carlos Berba, Vic Lecaros, Rey Catapang, Agnes Buenaventura, Joey de la Cruz, Gene Calonge, Gene Arias, Jojo Sanchez, Benny Reyes, Boying Lallana, Trichie Berba, Eugene Reyes, Bong Cayabyab, Mike Anderson, Alex Brillantes, Gambhir Bhatta, Kay Mohlman, Virgilio Labrador, Phineas Alburo, Emil Bolongaita, Daute Cadiz, Ernie Ordonez, Victor Ordonez, Leslie Alcantara, Hayati Ismail and Leela Vengadasalam.

Individuals from many organisations also made this book possible. They include the Office of the Philippine President, National Economic and Development Authority, Philippine Airlines, City of Baguio, Philippine Department of Finance, Philippine Department of Tourism, Philippine Department of Trade and Industry, Philippine Department of the Interior and Local Government, De La Salle University (Manila), Philippine Embassy in Washington, DC and Singapore, Overseas Workers Welfare Administration, National University of Singapore, World Bank, International Monetary Fund, Asian Development Bank, Asia-Pacific Economic Cooperation, APEC Foundation of the Philippines, International Labour Organisation, United Nations Development Programme, University of the Philippines, Asian Institute of Management, Subic Bay Management Authority, Clark Development Corporation, Nanyang Technological University (Singapore), Design International Selections, San Miguel

Corporation, Institute On Governance (Canada), Institute of Southeast Asian Studies, Congress of the Philippines, US State Department, US Information Service in Manila and Singapore, Price Waterhouse (Philippines), Castillo Laman Tan Pantaleon & San Jose Law Firm, Canadian International Development Agency, and National Hardware (Singapore).

Introduction

As in any other country, succeeding in business in the Philippines requires doing your homework diligently. This means acquiring a keen working knowledge of not only the Philippine business sector or product market that you intend to invest in, but also the unique underlying features of the society and culture. This book will serve as a guide to initiating, harnessing and maintaining strategic relationships with both the private and public sectors, and the business community you will encounter in the country.

Starting out with the business outlook, the first chapter provides an update on recent efforts by Philippine Government officials and corporate leaders to leave behind the country's tainted past and strive towards greater economic growth. This chapter's sub-sections on the international network of partnerships at the bilateral, regional, multilateral and global levels show just where the country stands in terms of regional and global trade networks.

A total understanding of Philippine trade and business practices would not be possible without a trip back in time to the colourful past of this former Spanish and American colony. Chapter 2 highlights many critical events that shaped the nation, from the days of early trading in the precolonial period to the martial law years of the Marcos regime then finally to the days of redemocratisation and market liberalisation under the Aquino and Ramos administrations. The events that turned the "Pearl of the Orient" into the "sick man of Asia" and finally into an economic powerhouse it is today make for a fascinating and invaluable read.

We move from history to politics as chapter 3 examines the workings of the government. The three governmental branches—executive, legislative and judicial—are discussed, as is the role of the military. There is also a special focus on the government agencies you would encounter as you make your way through the necessary red tape. Not forgotten are other players in the political scene, such as political parties, interest groups and the church.

We get down to business in the next chapter as we look at how to go about getting your business operations off the ground. Here we discuss the how, what and wherefore: how do I organise a business enterprise?; how do I form a Philippine corporation?; what are the investment procedures and requirements that I need to know?; where do I go for immigration and customs clearances?; and other burning questions that a potential investor has to address.

In fact, one of these questions would probably be: where should I channel my investment? In chapter 5, four leading niches are offered for consideration. For starters, there are the production and manufacturing possibilities at the two former American military installations—Subic Bay and Clark Field—that have been converted into bustling freeports and special economic zones. Opportunities also abound in public-private partnerships in the fast-growing infrastructure, power and utilities sectors. Investors tired of Metropolitan Manila can also expand their operations to investment centres emerging in the various regions of the country. Finally, there is the tourism sector, with fresh investment possibilities in resorts and transportation facilities. All four niches offer attractive built-in perks and incentives.

Chapter 6 focuses on management matters. The Filipino management style is examined and you get an insight into the nature of the employer-employee relationship. The role of women in business and society is also discussed at length for a better understanding of the vital role they play in the country's economy. The last chapter provides an opportunity for the reader to get to know more about the Filipino people—their culture, customs, language and education. After all, it is surely not enough just knowing about the economic and political systems. Getting to know the Filipinos and what makes them tick is just as important for a successful business venture in the Philippines.

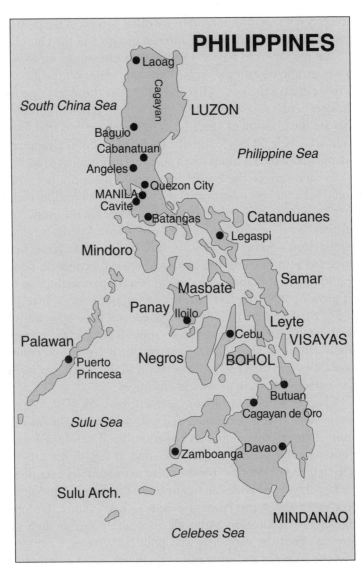

Map of the Philippines

CHAPTER 1

Outlook for the Philippines

Three Commandments for Potential Investors

1. Thou shall not regard the Philippines as the "sick man of Asia" any more.
2. Thou shall seriously look at the Philippines as a strategic launching pad for thy business in Asia.
3. Thou shall not allow thyself to be left behind as the Philippine bandwagon zooms by.

— Finance Secretary Roberto de Ocampo

Leaving Behind the Past

Once upon a time, international investors and companies ignored investment opportunities in the Philippines. Many did not want to have anything to do with the country—and for good reason.

Ironically, even local Filipino entrepreneurs were sceptical about the general outlook for the economy. While neighbouring nations were opening their economies to global trade and investments, the Philippines was doing just about the opposite. The two paths that the Philippines and its neighbours chose to take led to two different results. While East Asian miracle economies led the world into an Asia-Pacific century, Philippines was labelled the "sick man of Asia". This was hard for the Filipino pride to swallow as the Philippine economy was second to Japan in Asia during the 1960s.

Of late, however, the Philippine economy has shown signs of a long-awaited renaissance. Finally, Filipinos seem determined to leave behind their tainted past and move forward to let the country regain its title as "Pearl of the Orient". In 1996 alone, thousands of

11

small to large enterprises set up shop in the country, pouring in more than US$1 billion in investments. Ten new banks have established consumer branches in the Philippines in the past few years. Less well-known has been the establishment in Manila of several offices of foreign banks to serve capital markets. Many business ventures are contemplating jumping on the bandwagon.

Why is there a sudden surge in business and investor confidence? This is because governmental changes have facilitated export-oriented and investment-led growth policies. Steps taken include trade and industry liberalisation, tax restructuring and an improved debt management.

The government also removed restrictions on foreign exchange transactions. Despite fears to the contrary, this has produced a net inflow of new foreign exchange from old and new sources. For instance, overseas Filipino workers from North America, Western Europe and the Middle East, who were wary of repatriating money back to the country, either held on to their foreign exchange or invested them elsewhere.

The increasing flow of domestic and foreign investments have created many jobs, some resulting from a high demand for goods and services. The effects can be seen in the liberalisation of employment in the shipping, aviation and telecommunications sectors over the past few years.

In telecommunications, new telephone and cable TV providers have created thousands of new jobs. Even old service providers have had to hire new workers to meet the demand for interconnections between the newcomers. A better communications system has improved the climate for investment and business. With improved rural communications, new areas for entrepreneurship have opened up outside the Metropolitan Manila area. Outlying agricultural communities are already reaping the benefits. For the first time, through cellular phone networks, rural farmers have instantaneous access to the latest information on the price of their goods. Some of the oldest and most

San Miguel: Going Regional and Even Global

San Miguel Corporation is the largest publicly listed food, beverage and packaging company in the Philippines. Founded in 1890 as a small brewery, the company and its subsidiaries today generate about 4% of the Philippines' GNP and about 5% of government tax revenues.

The company's strategic goals of consolidating domestic leadership and international expansion are the cornerstones of its recent major initiatives in pursuit of its vision to be Asia's best. San Miguel's flagship product, San Miguel Beer, holds an 80% share of the Philippine market. It is among the world's largest-selling beers and one of the top three brands in Asia.

San Miguel now has five breweries in the Philippines, one brewery in Vietnam and a joint venture brewery in Indonesia. In China, where it has the most extensive beer operations outside the Philippines, San Miguel has opened three breweries: two in Guangdong province and one in Baoding City near Beijing. The Hong Kong brewery, recently relocated in the New Territories, now counts as the fourth brewery in its China operations. San Miguel opened 11 new sales offices in China in the first half of 1997, bringing the total number to 27 sales offices, with two more expected to open before the end of the year.

In soft drinks, the company is the second largest investor in Coca-Cola Amatil (CCA), the largest Coca-Cola bottler outside the United States. Through CCA, San Miguel's soft drinks interests span the Asia-Pacific, Australian and European markets, with a consumer base of 450 million. Through partnerships with international companies, San Miguel has gained access to the latest technologies and expertise. It has long-standing partnerships with the Coca-Cola Company and Nestle of Switzerland. San Miguel has 45% equity in Nestle Philippines, Inc., which produces, among others, liquid and powdered milk, food seasonings, and ice cream. San Miguel's other successful joint ventures are with the New Zealand Dairy Board, Yamamura Glass, Fuso Machine and Mould Manufacturing Company and Rengo Corporation of Japan, Ball Corporation of the United States, United Distillers of the United Kingdom, and Conservera Campofrio of Spain.

conservative companies are also sporting a more aggressive and global outlook—a show of confidence in the mother economy and the economic prospects beyond.

The unequivocal results of these changes testify to the benefits of a market-oriented economic system. In 1994 and 1995, the Philippines achieved national budget surpluses for the first time in 20 years. Inflation and interest rates went down dramatically. While exports from the region slowed down, exports from the Philippines continue to grow, up from 14% growth in 1993 to almost 30% in 1995.

Foreign direct investment inflows have risen by an annual average of about 48% between 1992 and 1995. Net investment inflows in the first half of 1996 increased at an astonishing 178% in the first half of 1995. The overall economy grew by almost 6% in 1995 and is expected to expand by 7% in 1996. This is clearly seen in the country's 5.6% growth in 1997 despite the region's financial crisis, which practically devastated some of its Southeast Asian neighbours.

Role of Local Capital

The Philippine Board of Investments (BOI) states that local capital accounts for the bulk of equity investments into the country. Local investments are concentrated mostly in export production while foreign capital is increasingly dominant in domestic production.

BOI-approved Equity Investments (in billion pesos)

	1994	1995	1996
No. of Projects	536	285	463
Total Equity Investments	87.90	57.53	116.38
Local	54.63	23.65	91.00
Foreign	33.28	33.88	25.38

Source: Board of Investments

An exhibition launched by President Ramos in 1997 on the Pandanan Wreck 1414. It reflects the country's vital role (past and present) in regional trade.

A Statistical Overview of the Philippine Economy

	1994	1995	1996
Gross Domestic Product (% Growth)	4.4	4.8	5.7
Agriculture	3.1	0.8	3.1
Industry	5.8	7.0	6.3
Services	4.2	5.0	6.5
Gross Domestic Investment (% of GDP)	24.1	22.2	24.8
Gross Domestic Savings (% of GDP)	18.0	16.6	19.8
Inflation (% change in CPI)	9.0	8.1	8.4
Merchandise Exports (US$ m)	13,483	17,447	20,543
Increase from Previous Year (%)	18.5	29.4	17.7
Merchandise Imports (US$ m)	21,333	26,391	31,756
Increase from Previous Year (%)	21.2	23.7	20.3
External Debt (US$ b)	37.1	37.8	NA
Debt Service Ratio as % of Exports	15.0	13.8	10.3
Foreign Direct Investments (US$ m)	1,591	1,459	1,408
Foreign Portfolio Investment (US$ m)	3,685	4,488	8,006
Government Budget Allocation (%)			
Infrastructure	11	11	10
Debt Service	36	38	28
Social Welfare	0.3	0.4	0.3
Education	11	14	14
Defence	7	7	10
Leading Manufacturing Sectors (US$ m)			
Food Manufactures	6,214	6,853	7,992
Products of Petroleum and Coal	1,306	1,435	1,576
Leading Export Markets (US$ m)			
USA	5,143	6,132	6,966
Japan	2,024	2,733	3,668
Singapore	709	994	1,224
Foreign Investment Sources (US$ m)			
USA	680	628	NA
Hong Kong	288	NA	280
Taiwan	265	NA	NA
Foreign Investment Sectors (US$ m)			
Manufacturing	1,282	1,317	300
Energy-related	823	35	30
Public Utilities	132	357	200

A closer look at these investments reveals that the increase has been due mainly to a surge in portfolio investments and rising loans. Portfolio investments, considered less risky for foreign investors, are short-term capital inflows that take advantage of profitable stock market speculation and the high interest rates of Treasury bills (T-bills). However, the Philippine Government is trying to encourage more long-term ventures through various investment perks and benefits.

Overseas Filipinos

There over six million overseas Filipinos living or working in more than 100 countries. The type of jobs they undertake vary widely, from being domestic helpers to corporate managers.

This Filipino diaspora is not a new phenomenon, having started even during the Spanish administration of the archipelago in the 16th century. In the past, the Philippine economy was unable to absorb the large numbers of individuals that emerged from its educational system.

This situation was intensified further by a labour export policy of the Marcos administration in the 1970s. The Philippines continues to reap the dividends of overseas Filipinos through the billions of dollars of foreign exchange remittances pumped into the economy annually through the banking system. In 1995, the Migrant Workers and Overseas Filipinos Act (Republic Act 8042) was passed into law by Congress. The law primarily provided increased protective measures and welfare benefits to what former President Corazon Aquino called "the unsung heroes and heroines" of the Philippines.

Political Stability

On the political front, the Philippines seems to have made significant gains. The government has achieved peace with leftist and rightist rebels through reconciliation, negotiations, talks and compromises. Terrorist threats from groups like the Communist

Party of the Philippines, New People's Army and the Moro secessionist movement in Muslim Mindanao have been reduced because of on-going peace talks and reconciliation meetings.

However, the downside to wealth and prosperity is the alarming increase in the number of violent crimes, especially in Metro Manila. Some of these crimes are committed by former law enforcement officials who run operations ranging from kidnappings-for-ransom to bank heists and drug syndicates. In 1996, the Hong Kong-based Political and Economic Risk Consultancy (PERC) rated the Philippines as one of the most unsafe countries in Asia to visit.

However, the situation now has changed dramatically, thanks to strong directives from the president and serious action from police agencies and the courts.

Social Issues

Philippine development can only be considered successful if the government is able to facilitate wealth-sharing among the people. More importantly, the fruits of development must be within the reach of the economically disadvantaged and the poverty-stricken.

The Philippines will soon join the ranks of its East Asian neighbours. However, it needs to catch up not only by maintaining a robust economy but also by reducing income inequality and poverty among the people.

There is still a great divide between the "haves" and the "have nots". In the major cities, street beggars, urban slums and squatter settlements are still a common sight.

In the countryside, poor disbursement of funds due to political squabbling is hampering the implementation of land redistribution and rural infrastructure, which are key elements of the development of the land reform programme.

A perennial challenge to Philippine public policy planners is creating enough social and economic rewards for all Filipinos in a nation with one of the highest population growth rates in the

Social Indicators for the Philippines

Area (approximately)	300,000 sq km (115,600 sq m)
Population	69.7 million
Population Growth	2.3%
Urban Population	46%
Per capita GDP (real)	US$3,020
Per capita GNP (nominal)	US$1,265
Life Expectancy	67
Literacy Rate	95%
People per Telephone	38.6

East Asian region. From 1965 to 1974, the population of the Philippines grew at a rate of 3.1% annually, one of the highest in the world, with a ranking of 33 out of 180 countries.

More than half the rural population are poor and need the disbursement from the government in order to facilitate development projects that would in turn help change their age-old tenurial status. Many village communities in the provinces are still unable to meet basic human needs like access to potable water, toilets and immunisation services. Approximately 40% of households in 21 provinces still do not have access to toilet facilities and close to 40% of households in 11 provinces do not have access to a safe water supply. High rates of malnutrition, especially among children, still exist in 12 provinces. Ironically, some of these provinces are the most resource-rich in the country.

In response to these concerns, the Ramos administration has launched an all-out war that seeks to address population, health, poverty and other social issues. A development master plan, Philippines 2000, is one of the key plans to eradicating these social concerns. Transcending all political and administrative time frames, it envisages an improved quality of life for all Filipinos as well as the attainment of the status of a Newly Industrialising Country (NIC) by the year 2000.

Thus, this is the battle cry of the Medium-Term Philippine Development Plan (MTPDP) for 1993–1998, which Philippine President Fidel V. Ramos launched on 25 February 1993. Philippines 2000 is a two-pronged approach that calls for an economic development programme anchored on "global competitiveness" and "people empowerment". World competitiveness or global excellence calls for a situation in which the Philippines is able to produce products that are competitive not only at the regional level but also on the world market.

People empowerment advocates the enabling of ordinary Filipinos to take control over every aspect of their lives—their livelihood, politics and culture. In essence, Philippines 2000 endeavours to make the country the next investment, trade and tourism centre of Asia and the Pacific. The country's location at the crossroads of Southeast Asia makes it an ideal place for investors.

The Philippines, through its Department of Trade and Industry (DTI), promotes investments and agri-industrial development in order to enhance global competitiveness as well as create more jobs and wealth for Filipinos. The 1997 target of PHP450 billion of domestic investment and job generation will be achieved through industry expansion, integration and dispersal.

Industry expansion will involve the restoration of industry capacity, expansion of existing capacities and the establishment of new facilities. Industry integration will require the establishment, modernisation and rehabilitation of strategic basic industries.

Government investment and trade agencies will also require the development of competitive small and medium enterprises (SMEs), enhancement of agro-industrial linkages and the operation of the Backward Linkages Programme. Industry dispersal will be undertaken through joint initiatives comprising the local governments and the private sector. Both sectors will be actively involved in the creation of a business-friendly environment in the Philippines.

A view of the Rizal Monument as the sun sets in Manila Bay. With over six million of its people overseas, the country's global network extends far beyond its shores.

The operation of Regional Growth Centres (RGCs) and the devolution of services to local units will also help in the dispersal of industries to the various regions of the country. The Trade and Industry Department's Investment Priorities Plan, "Global Competition by Countryside Industry Dispersal", aims to sustain agri-industrial development in all the geographic regions of the Philippines through:

- Industrial restructuring for worldwide competition and expansion of capacities for production of goods and services for the domestic and export markets, including tourism
- Strong, productive and ecologically-sound links between agriculture and industry
- Higher income and better productivity

The labour force increases every year by an estimated 905,000 high school, vocational and college graduates. Due to an educational system that is designed to produce qualified graduates, investors will not find any problem in recruiting qualified workers.

The Philippines has one of the highest literacy rates in Asia, with 95% of its people able to read and write. The level of tertiary education is also one of the highest in the world. Foreign firms can readily avail themselves of the services of competent middle managerial and technical personnel at comparably lower costs than elsewhere in Asia. As workers, Filipinos demonstrate a high degree of industry and adaptability to different work environments. These characteristics, coupled with the fact that the average Filipino worker is highly literate and easily trainable, make them one of the most productive employees in Asia.

For economic growth and people empowerment, the Philippines promotes the generation of jobs and investments targeted especially at the country's vast rural areas by providing assistance to micro, small and medium enterprises. This is accomplished through livelihood projects that have liberal financing, technical training programmes, market development and institutional support.

Regional Growth Centres, which will be discussed in detail in chapter 5, are established in strategic locations throughout the country. Lucrative monetary and non-monetary incentives are also offered by both the national government agencies and the local government units to investors who choose to locate their companies in these areas.

Strengthening Bilateral, Regional and Global Ties

The Philippines has always had a reputation for carefully maintaining friendly bilateral, regional and global relations. It does this by actively pursuing an aggressive foreign policy that nurtures economic, political, social and cultural ties not just at the government-to-government level but also between the people of the Philippines and the peoples of the other countries. It is a member of many international organisations in the Asia-Pacific region and beyond.

Bilateral Ties

At the forefront of Philippine bilateral ties are two major economic powers: the United States and Japan. These two partners are prime destinations for goods and services exported from the Philippines. They are also primary sources of foreign investments and official development assistance in the form of grants and loans. People-to-people ties are also strong as the United States and Japan are major destinations for Filipinos, who leave the country for greener pastures either for a short period of time or permanently.

Together, Japan and the United States are the Philippines' main sources of direct equity investments. From 1973 to mid-1996, US and Japanese investments accounted for 53.3% of the total foreign direct equity investments in the country. Comparatively speaking, almost 87% of US investments come in as portfolio compared to Japan's investments (91%), which are more direct in nature. Taken cumulatively, although foreign investments in the country increased in the past three years, reaching 76% in 1995 to US$6.9 billion, more than two-thirds or US$5.3 billion are unproductive and speculative investments.

The United States

The Philippines has always had a special relationship with the government and people of the United States. For almost five decades, the Philippines was a colony of the United States, which established, among others, the country's educational system, legal process and political institutions. Filipinos have always been considered by their Asian neighbours as "brown Americans" because of their love for almost anything American, from food to fashion. Americans, on the other hand, will never forget the hundreds of thousands of Filipinos who fought side by side with the US Armed Forces in the Far East during World War II.

The US-Philippine relationship at present is based on shared democratic values and economic interests, common security concerns and a largely congruent view of the world. This was echoed by US Ambassador to the Philippines, Thomas C. Hubbard, in a January 1997 luncheon address, "The Philippines: Offering New Opportunities", to the American Chamber of Commerce in Hong Kong. He said US-Philippine bilateral relations had changed tremendously in recent years from one based on mutual security interests to one based on mutually beneficial trade and investment ties after the closure of the US military bases in the country in 1991. For instance, as the last annual audit and special pre-APEC investment survey of the American Chamber of Commerce showed, US firms planned to invest US$12 billion in the Philippines over the next five years.

Firms from the United States have participated actively in rebuilding the Philippines' power sector, strengthening its communications infrastructure, enhancing environmental protection and developing the burgeoning electronic sector, to name just a few. Their future participation in other ventures will continue to grow. The Armed Forces of the Philippines (AFP), for example, is looking towards modernisation. This is a window of opportunity that US firms seem poised to exploit as the United States is among the most competitive in the world in this area. In fact, US firms will find many opportunities in agricultural and forestry products, oil, minerals, construction, power generation, telecommunications, and the environment.

A high-ranking US State Department official notes that US firms have a distinct advantage: they have the know-how that can easily be transferred to an educated, English-speaking workforce. Interested US businesses will, therefore, do well in any of the aforesaid areas.

From 1946–1991, countries in Southeast Asia received more than US$43 billion worth of foreign development assistance (FDA) from the United States. This represents 19.8% of the total aid given to the Asian region (US$218.5 billion) and 11.1% of the total FDA provided by the US globally (US$389.7 billion). The Philippines received a whopping 15.7% of this amount. These came through the following programmes:

- Economic Aid: Agency for International Development (USAID), Food for Peace (PL 480), Peace Corps, Narcotics
- Military Aid: Military Assistance Programme Grants, Foreign Military Credit Financing, International Military Education and Training Programme, Transfers of Excess Defence Articles
- Other US loans and credits: Export-Import Bank Loans and short-term credit from the Department of Agriculture under the Credit Corporation Charter Act and Overseas Private Investment Corporation

Although the amount of military aid has diminished significantly after the US Armed Forces' withdrawal, the Philippines still benefits from many USAID-sponsored economic development assistance activities like the Governance and Local Democracy (GOLD), and Growth and Equity in Mindanao (GEM) projects. It is also one of the largest US Eximbank borrower in the Southeast Asian region.

Japan

Aside from its strong bilateral ties with the United States, the Philippines has built an equally solid relationship with the Japanese. Just as with its bonds with the United States, the Philippines has built a multi-faceted relationship with the "Land of the Rising Sun" that continues to strengthen with time. This can be seen in the flourishing trade and investment links between the two countries. For instance, in the first two quarters of 1995–1996, Japanese equity investments dominated all other registered foreign equity investments in the Philippines.

On the other hand, the Philippines has also become a primary market for Japanese exports. Demand for Japanese products, from consumer electronics to heavy equipment, has risen sharply in the last decade. Aside from trade and investment links, people-to-people relations between the Philippines and Japan are strong. Officially, there are close to 85,000 Filipinos residing in Japan. In turn, according to Japan's Ministry of Foreign Affairs, its 1995 statistics show that there are more than 4,000 Japanese nationals who are registered as Philippine residents.

Unlike the United States which provides three types of bilateral foreign development assistance to the Philippines, Japan concentrates on providing the country with economic loans and grants, called the Official Development Assistance (ODA). Japan does not provide any form of military aid because of its wartime record in the region, its constitutional limitations on military-related activities, and its efforts to project itself as a pacifist nation and an economic power. ODA grants to the Philippines consist of direct project grants and technical cooperation programmes while

ODA loans are made up of project and non-project loans, and debt rescheduling. Close to 80% (US$17.6 billion) of total Japanese ODA to Southeast Asia from 1971–1993 had gone to three out of 10 recipient countries—Indonesia, the Philippines and Thailand. The Philippines received US$6.3 billion of ODA loans, more than 23% of the region's total.

Other Bilateral Ties

The Philippines also has strong and enduring bilateral, political, economic, social and cultural ties with its neighbours in Southeast Asia, East Asia and other countries. For instance, Singapore was the Philippines' third-largest export market and Thailand its fourth-largest foreign investor in 1995. Major investors also include Hong Kong, Taiwan, Saudi Arabia and the United Kingdom. Their investments are mainly concentrated in the manufacturing, energy, and public utilities sectors. The Philippines also benefits from many bilateral technical cooperation and technical assistance projects, which transfer much needed knowledge and tools to the country.

Overall, portfolio inflows jumped by close to 80%, from US$4.49 billion in 1995 to US$8.01 billion in 1996. Meanwhile, medium and long-term loans increased by more than 60%, from US$3.93 billion to US$6.33 billion.

The Philippines maintains these important relationships through a network of more than 70 diplomatic and consular missions staffed with foreign service officers, who are always ready to assist any potential investor. In countries without a Philippine mission, an honorary consul is usually present to provide advice. Reciprocally, the country plays host to more than 80 diplomatic and consular missions representing countries in Africa, North and South America, Asia, Europe, and Australia. Bilateral business councils are also common arrangements between the private business sectors of the Philippines and a partner country.

Regional Ties

The Philippines plays an active role in the workings of many major regional and sub-regional organisations like the Association of Southeast Asian Nations (ASEAN), the Asia-Pacific Economic Cooperation (APEC), the Asian Development Bank (ADB), the Asia-Europe Meeting (ASEM), the Brunei, Indonesia, Malaysia, Philippines-East ASEAN Growth Area (BIMP-EAGA), Pacific Basin Economic Council (PBEC) and the Pacific Economic Cooperation Council (PECC). It shares the sentiments of leaders within the region that close cooperation and mutual understanding, achieved through active participation in these international organisations, are the best ways to move forward.

Association of Southeast Asian Nations (ASEAN) was established on 8 August 1967 in Bangkok with the signing of the Bangkok Declaration by the five original member countries, namely the Philippines, Indonesia, Malaysia, Singapore and Thailand. Brunei Darussalam joined the grouping on 8 January 1984 while Vietnam became the seventh member on 28 July 1995. Laos and Myanmar were admitted in July 1997.

The Bangkok Declaration united the ASEAN member countries in a joint effort to promote economic cooperation and the welfare of the peoples in the region. It set out guidelines and defined the aims of the organisation. ASEAN nations came together with three main objectives: to promote the economic, social and cultural development of the region through cooperative programmes, to safeguard the political and economic stability of the region against big power rivalry, and to serve as a forum for the resolution of intra-regional differences. As one of its founding members, the Philippines plays an active role in the affairs of this regional organisation through the ASEAN Secretariat and its many working committees.

The Philippines is a strong supporter of the ASEAN Free Trade Area (AFTA), which is a multilateral preferential trading arrangement among member states. It acts as a stimulus to the strengthening of economic resilience and the development of the national economies by expanding investment and production opportunities, trade, and foreign exchange earnings.

Common Effective Preferential Tariff (CEPT) is an agreed effective tariff, preferential to ASEAN that is to be applied to goods originating from ASEAN countries and have been identified for inclusion in the CEPT scheme. The Philippines is a signatory to many ASEAN agreements like the ASEAN Industrial Complementation Agreement, the ASEAN Emergency Grain Reserve Agreement and the ASEAN Fisheries Cooperation. The Philippines is also an active participant in many ASEAN trade and investment programmes like the ASEAN Industrial Joint Ventures and the ASEAN Agricultural Development Planning Centre.

Asia-Pacific Economic Cooperation (APEC) was formed in 1989 in response to the growing interdependence among Asia-Pacific economies. Aside from the Philippines, APEC members include: Australia, Brunei, Canada, Chile, China, Hong Kong, Indonesia, Japan, South Korea, Malaysia, Mexico, New Zealand, Papua New Guinea, Singapore, Taiwan, Thailand and the United States. It began as an informal dialogue group with limited participation, but it has since become the primary regional vehicle for promoting open trade and practical economic cooperation. Its goal is to advance Asia-Pacific economic dynamism and sense of community.

APEC's 18-member economies had a combined Gross Domestic Product of over US$13 trillion in 1995, approximately 55% of total world income and 46% of global trade. The Philippines has shown its strong commitment to this Asia-Pacific grouping by hosting the 1996 annual meeting of leaders in Manila and Subic Bay. During the meeting, APEC outlined and adopted the Manila Action Plan for APEC (or MAPA 96), which is the blueprint for the journey towards free trade and investment across the region by the year 2010 for developed economies and 2020 for developing ones.

According to a US representative, APEC was an impressive showcase of Philippine political and economic confidence. At Blake Island off the coast of Washington State in 1993, APEC outlined the above vision. In Bogor and Osaka, the vision was given a definite form and direction.

In 1996, APEC needed to deliver on its commitment to advance free trade and investment in the region. In one impressive document, MAPA 1996, the Philippines and other APEC countries outlined concrete steps to realise that goal. With MAPA produced under Philippine chairmanship, APEC moved from vision to action. Philippine leadership also gave new definition to APEC's efforts to strengthen economic and technical cooperation. President Ramos set the tone by calling on APEC to engender "a spirit of common problem solving". Through its new Framework for Strengthening Economic Cooperation and Development, APEC has agreed to work together to tackle the "roadblocks" in each economy that limit its ability to grow.

Asian Development Bank (ADB) is a multilateral development finance institution that consists of 56 member countries. The ADB promotes the economic and social progress of its developing member countries in the Asia-Pacific region. The ADB began its operations in December 1966 with its headquarters in Manila. It is owned by the governments of 40 countries in the region and 16 countries outside the region.

During the past 30 years, the ADB has maintained its role as a catalyst in promoting the development of the region. The ADB's principal functions are to:

- Make loans and equity investments for the economic and social advancement of developing member countries

- Provide technical assistance for the preparation and execution of development projects and programmes, and advisory services
- Promote investment of public and private capital for development purposes
- Respond to requests for assistance in coordinating development policies and plans of developing member countries

The ADB pays special attention to the needs of the smaller or less-developed countries and gives priority to regional, sub-regional and national projects and programmes, which will contribute to the economic growth of the region and promote cooperation.

Asia-Europe Meeting (ASEM) is an annual summit between government officials from Asia and Europe. The first ASEM meeting in March 1996 was indeed a historic occasion since it brought to Thailand leaders from two continents, representing 25 countries and the European Commission. Aside from the Philippines, participants in the ASEM included the heads of state and the governments of nine Asian nations and 15 European nations, and the president of the European Commission.

The initiative for ASEM grew from the recognised need to strengthen the link between Asian and European countries. While the Trans-Pacific and Trans-Atlantic links (through the APEC forum and the Group of Seven respectively) appear to be strong, ties between Asia and Europe have not been fully developed. ASEM helped strengthen this link as well as foster closer ties between the three main centres of economic growth, namely Asia, Europe and North America.

ASEM seeks to strengthen the economic ties between Asia and Europe by taking advantage of the existing complementarity and developing synergies that would promote greater economic growth and development. Another important goal is promoting more trade and investments between the two regions through trade and investment liberalisation and facilitation among the participating countries.

The above initiatives are intended to complement existing efforts at achieving an open, rules-based trading system that comes within the framework of the World Trade Organisation (WTO). In addition, ASEM encourages Asian and European businesses and private sectors to strengthen their cooperation through increased contact, joint ventures and technology transfer.

Brunei, Indonesia, Malaysia, Philippines-East ASEAN Growth Area (BIMP-EAGA) was an idea mooted by Philippine President Ramos. BIMP-EAGA stretches from west Kalimantan to Irian Jaya in the east, a sprawling area covering 3,500 km in length and 2,000 km in width. BIMP-EAGA joins two other sub-regional cooperative arrangements in Southeast Asia: the Indonesia-Malaysia-Singapore Growth Triangle (IMS-GT) and the Indonesia-Malaysia-Thailand Growth Triangle (IMT-GT). BIMP-EAGA was formally set up in March 1994 to increase much-needed cross-border trade and investment among these four ASEAN neighbours.

The Philippines is interested in getting potential business people into the southern provinces comprising Mindanao (the country's second largest island), which has remained largely untapped because of past civil strife. However, relatively successful peace initiatives between the government and the Moro separatists have emboldened Philippine leaders to try a renewed economic development approach.

The Asian Development Bank has just completed a study identifying areas for trade and investment cooperation in the Philippines and the region. An East ASEAN Business Council (EABC) was set up in November 1994. It consists of the various regional chambers of commerce found in this region.

APEC Business Advisory Council (ABAC) is a forum for senior business leaders of APEC. In November 1995, APEC economic leaders established ABAC as a permanent forum to advise them and other APEC officials on issues of interest to business. ABAC also responds to requests from various APEC fora for information on business-related issues or the business perspective on specific areas of cooperation.

ABAC is made up of three senior business persons appointed by APEC economic leaders from each APEC member economy. ABAC seeks to represent the broad spectrum of business interests; one member from each economy generally comes from a small or medium-sized company.

The chairmanship of ABAC rotates according to the country that chairs APEC. ABAC activities are now fully self-funded, although the APEC Central Fund contributed to its start-up expenses in its first year of operation.

ABAC will consider new initiatives in 1997 but its main focus will be on the concrete achievement of business-friendly proposals already issued, not in generating new proposals. ABAC has set up three sectoral committees to implement this work plan, covering cross-border flows, finance/investment/infrastructure issues and economic cooperation, a special committee on small and medium-sized companies, and a steering committee for the review of the Manila Action Plan for APEC.

Pacific Economic Cooperation Council (PECC) is a tripartite, non-governmental organisation devoted to promoting economic cooperation in the Pacific Rim. PECC brings together government officials, academics and business people to share perspectives and expertise so that broad-based answers to the economic problems of the region can be found. The PECC was founded in 1980 and is the only private observer body in the APEC ministerial forum. Aside from the Philippines, other countries involved in the PECC are Australia, Brunei, Canada, Chile, China, Colombia, Hong Kong, Indonesia, Japan, South Korea, Malaysia, Mexico, New Zealand, Peru, Russia, Singapore, Taiwan, Thailand, the United States, Vietnam and the Pacific Island Nations.

The Philippines supports PECC activities, such as organising seminars and workshops, and conducting studies on issues pertaining to capital and financial markets, fisheries development and cooperation, human resource development, science and technology, transportation, telecommunications, and tourism.

Pacific Basin Economic Council (PBEC) is an association of business leaders from across the Pacific. It promotes the expansion of trade and investment through open markets. Founded in 1967, PBEC serves as a forum through which regional business leaders create new business relationships and address emerging issues in the Pacific and global economies. Member companies are affiliated with PBEC through its 17 member committees in Australia, Canada, Chile, China, Colombia, Fiji, Hong Kong, Japan, South Korea, Malaysia, Mexico, New Zealand, Peru, the Philippines, Russia, Taiwan and the United States. PBEC assists in the economic growth of the region through programmes aimed at increasing understanding and by encouraging networking and business relationships among its members. PBEC supports open markets, advocates the reduction of trade and investment barriers, and encourages economic cooperation based on the shared interests of its members.

Other Multilateral Linkages

The Philippines is heavily involved in the Asia Productivity Organisation (APO), Colombo Plan, ASEAN Inter-Parliamentary Organisation (AIPO), Asia Pacific Parliamentary Union, Committee for Coordination of Joint Prospecting for Mineral Resources in Asian Offshore Areas (CCOP/East Asia), Asian and Pacific Coconut Community (APCC), and ASEAN sub-groupings like the ASEAN Regional Forum (ARF), ASEAN Fund and the ASEAN Reinsurance Corporation.

The Philippines is an active member of international organisations like the United Nations and its numerous agencies, such as the United Nations Development Programme (UNDP), the United Nations Industrial Development Organisation (UNIDO), the United Nations Economic and Social Commission for Asia and the Pacific (UNESCAP), the United Nations Conference on Trade and Development (UNCTAD), and the Food and Agriculture Organisation (FAO).

The Philippines also actively endorses many International Labour Organisation (ILO) conventions, resolutions and standards. It is represented in the World Bank Group, that is, the International Bank for Reconstruction and Development (IBRD), the International Finance Corporation (IFC), the Multilateral Investment Guarantee Agency (MIGA) and the International Development Association (IDA), as well as its sister organisation, the International Monetary Fund (IMF).

The country subscribes to the guidelines, policies, procedures and decisions of the WTO, the World Health Organisation (WHO), the Customs Cooperation Council (CCC) and the International Court of Justice (ICJ). It is also a signatory to the following international economic agreements: Intellectual Property Rights (IPR), Globalised Comprehensive Import Supervision Scheme (GCISS) and Cairns Group.

The Philippines is also home to the regional and country offices of the Delegation of the European Communities, the Regional Delegation for the Pacific of the International Committee of the Red Cross (ICRC), the Regional Mission in East Asia and the Pacific of the International Finance Corporation (IFC), the International Monetary Fund (IMF), the International Organisation for Migration (IOM), the International Rice Research Institute (IRRI), the United Nations System, World Bank, and the WHO Regional Office for the Western Pacific.

35

CHAPTER 2

Philippine History
for the Business Person

One cannot fully comprehend the workings of Philippine trade, investment and business practices without examining the country's interesting history, especially from a business person's perspective. The lethargy or vibrancy that characterises many important sectors in the economy cannot be explained without reference to these underpinnings. The foundations of the Philippines political, social, economic and cultural institutions were laid down during its rich and colourful past. Hence, understanding the Filipino business heritage may be the key to a long-lasting commercial venture. Impress your contacts, clients or colleagues with your grasp of the country's vibrant history.

Precolonial Economic System

Even before the arrival of the first Europeans, the Philippines had a thriving economic system that revolved around an inter-island trading system. Socio-political relations between *barangays* or village communities, consisting of between 30 and 100 families, facilitated a vibrant exchange of goods among inhabitants of the many islands. Many boats from the Visayan and Mindanao islands frequented *barangays* in Luzon with basic necessities. Economic relations were strengthened through contacts and agreements. Intermarriages, usually arranged by members of two ruling families, created important kinship ties among trading communities. Agricultural goods traded included rice, coconuts, sugar cane, bananas, and other fruit and vegetables. Early non-agricultural industries involved livestock-raising, pottery, boat-building, mining, weaving and fishing.

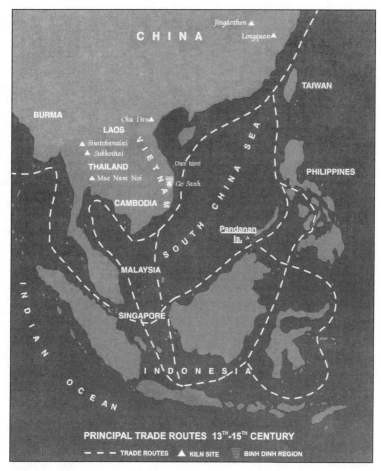

Map of the early trading routes in the region. The Philippines had a flourishing trade with the countries of the region. Trade among the islands of the Philippines also posted healthy results.

In terms of international trade, ships from China, India, the Middle East and other parts of Southeast Asia arrived with exotic cargoes. The long voyages over thousands of miles of rough seas were propelled by strong monsoon winds blowing south-east towards the islands of the Philippines. With the help of the northwesterly wind flow, the Chinese, Malay and Arab traders brought with them goods from the Philippines, which they traded in China, India and mainland Southeast Asia. With no paper currencies to exchange, barter became the main mode of commercial transaction. Goods were priced in gold and other precious metals. A high degree of trust and honesty were integral components of both the local and foreign trading systems.

Pandanan Wreck 1414

The discovery of this pre-Spanish shipwreck off the coast of Pandanan Island in Balabac, Palawan confirms the vital role that the Philippines played in the regional travel and trade business. It proves that in the 15th century, merchant vessels were already sailing through Southeast Asia, charting new routes for trade and commerce and venturing into the unknown.

The *Pandanan* highlights the fact that early maritime merchants and explorers set off for the Philippine archipelago's southernmost tip in search of a prized trading good—the south sea pearl, a much sought-after commodity then and now. The south sea pearl is one of the country's national gems. After all, the country's nickname is "Pearl of the Orient".

The *Pandanan* was discovered in 1993 by divers harvesting pearls. The wreck turned out to be a remarkably preserved mid-15th century Chinese merchant vessel that yielded some 5,000 pieces of priceless Chinese, Vietnamese and Thai porcelain, ceramics, and artifacts from a little-known period in history. It is believed that a strong monsoon typhoon had sunk the ship.

Source: Department of Tourism

Colonial Economy (1521–1946)

For more that 400 years, the Philippines played host to colonial administrators—the Spaniards for 300 years, the Americans for 50 years and the Japanese for three years. During their stay, these foreigners benefited heavily from the existing inter-island and regional trading arrangements. The colonisers linked the country to an even larger economic system from what it had known.

Spanish Administration

According to most history books, the first Westerner to set foot on Philippine soil was Ferdinand Magellan who named the islands after his benefactor, King Philip of Spain. As soon as they were able to set up a permanent presence in Manila by the late 16th century, the Spaniards immediately went about creating a centrally planned economic system. Politically, the Spaniards were also the first to establish a system that unified the country's tribal settlements scattered in its numerous islands. To establish and maintain control over its possession, the Spanish administrators provided incentives to select groups.

With the blessings of the Crown, Spanish administrators awarded royal grants of land (*encomiendas*) to its soldiers (*conquistadores*) and the religious orders (*friars*) for their role in Spain's conquest, pacification and Christianisation campaigns. By royal decree, these two groups of beneficiaries were given the privilege and authority to collect tribute (*buwis*) from the inhabitants of their *encomiendas*. Payments were made in cash or in kind.

Aside from these personal tributes, natives (*indios*) were subjected to other forms of financial and service requirements by the central government, for example, compulsory sale of goods (*bandala*), church tax (*sanctorum*), forced labour (*polo*) and personal identity papers (*cedula*). The *encomienda* and taxation systems were effective revenue-generating schemes, which made the Spanish Crown and their loyal followers wealthy.

Other than land grants, the king also gave favours (*merced*) to the *conquistadores* and their descendants. Regardless of educational or professional background, claimants to favours were able to bid for lucrative posts ranging from governor-general to provincial executives. Thus, a government position was treated as an investment from which a financial return could be gained. Moreover, the measly civil servant's pay that office holders received made it imperative for these early political elites to supplement their salaries through illegal means.

Over time, the well-off *conquistadores* and their descendants intermarried with the natives. Some *friars*, through illicit relationships with native women, fathered illegitimate children. These inter-racial unions produced a new elite class called the Spanish *mestizos*. Due to their Spanish lineage, members of this class were accorded higher status by Spanish authorities. Hence, when the high-ranking bureaucrats could not find any suitable "pure" Spaniards, they turned to these *mestizos*. They were recruited into public office to help administer the country and in return, were given the privilege to own land.

All throughout the Spanish era, Chinese merchants from mainland China frequented the Philippines' main towns and cities, trading goods from other parts of the Orient for locally-produced items, such as foodstuffs, fabrics, gold, pearl and ironware.

According to historical records, between 30 and 40 Chinese junks came to the Philippines annually. When the Spaniards settled permanently in the country, they could do little to change these long-established trading ties. Eventually, Chinese merchants became an integral part of the lucrative galleon trade. Manila became an important trans-shipment point for goods from China to Mexico and Peru. Spanish authorities in Madrid turned a blind eye to the Chinese traders' activities as they believed that Spain could benefit more from the trade. Some of them even argued that the Manila-Acapulco galleon trade was not helping the Philippine economy. However, overseas Spaniards based in Manila and Acapulco, who were profiting greatly from the barter arrangements, largely ignored the views of those from Madrid.

With no restrictions on their presence, the Chinese established themselves more firmly in the archipelago through intermarriages with the locals. These cross-cultural unions gave birth to the Chinese *mestizo* class. Realising the futility of their efforts to curtail the trade and the growing presence of the *mestizos*, the Spanish authorities eventually granted them the right to buy and own land.

The global agricultural export boom, which began around the 1850s, increased the landholding value in the Philippines. Consequently, the Spanish and Chinese *mestizos* managed to amass more and more wealth and thus capital, which they used to buy more agricultural land and pay for their family's higher education. Hence, by the time the Americans deposed the Spaniards in 1898, the *mestizos* had already established themselves as the dominant force among landowners, with control over many parts of the local economy. They eventually came to be referred to as the landholding elites. Through the resulting *hacienda* system, these elites established massive plantations that produced coffee, sugar and spices for consumption in Europe. Spain utilised this economic system to exploit the resources of the Philippines until the late 1900s. The *hacienda* arrangement also gave birth to deep-seated patronage relationships between owners and their workers.

American Occupation

After losing the Spanish-American War, Spain was forced to cede the Philippines to the United States by the Treaty of Paris (1898). The Americans continued the concept of a centrally planned economic system, this time focusing on their own business interests. They saw the Philippines as a rich source of raw materials and a potential market for US goods and services.

In addition, the Philippines was an ideal jumping-off point for the larger Asian markets of China, Japan, India and the Middle East. US President William McKinley's "Benevolent Assimilation" Proclamation summed up the political and social imperatives for US colonisation of the people of the Philippine Islands. From a military standpoint, General Arthur MacArthur justified the strategic importance of the country by saying: "The Philippines are the finest group of islands in the world. Its strategic location is unexcelled by that of any other position in the globe … It affords a means of protecting American interests which with the very least output of physical power has the effect of a commanding position in itself to retard hostile action".

In other words, because of political, economic, social and security reasons, it became imperative for the United States to annex the country. During their occupation of the Philippines, the Americans attempted to break up the land held by the *mestizos* and the patronage system.

In 1902, the US authorities ordered the implementation of an agrarian reform programme. However, the reform failed partly because of the lack of supporting institutions and infrastructure, for example, credit facilities, and marketing and distribution systems.

Lacking institutional support, peasants fell prey to entrenched customs, naiveté, usury and other exploitative practices of the landlords, especially the *mestizos*. They were forced to sell their land back to the landlords at bargain prices. Eventually, the Americans decided to use these entrenched Filipino elites as local "partners" instead of going against them and their complex network of patron-client ties nurtured during the Spanish period. This linked the economic interest of the *mestizos* with the global trading network of the United States. The seeds of a special relationship were thus planted.

Perhaps the most critical feature of the US legacy was the creation of the commonwealth government, and the appointment and election of educated Filipinos as officials of the commonwealth. Since then, the *mestizos* have become a regular feature in the country's political scene. Those recruited were given broad powers to govern the country under the watchful eye of the US governor-general. Though laudable in its objectives, this democratisation gave the landholding elite influence over the administrative system. Because they had the wherewithal to invest in higher education, the landholding elites eventually came to dominate the commonwealth government. Thus, under American rule, the *mestizo* classes became entrenched economically and politically.

Corregidor canons now stand as a reminder of the country's colonial history.

World War II and Japan

From the European front, World War II spread to the Asia-Pacific region with the 7 December 1941 surprise bombing of Pearl Harbour in Hawaii by Japanese air and naval forces. As the only Asian possession of the United States, the Philippines became the next target. US military installations across the country were bombed. Manila was occupied in less than a month after the Pearl Harbour attack.

Under the command of General Douglas MacArthur, the United States Armed Forces in the Far East (USAFFE), comprising Filipino and US soldiers, set up their final stand in Bataan and subsequently Corregidor. However, the unrelenting sea and land barrages of the Japanese military forces drove the United States to surrender on 9 April 1942.

For three years, the United States lost control of its prized Asian territory and the Philippines became a Japanese-occupied republic. As a colony now in Japan's Greater East Asia Co-prosperity Sphere, the Philippines' centrally-oriented economic system was once again used to channel much-needed raw materials to another nation. Overall, however, the economy was at a standstill. Agricultural production declined. Trade and industry suffered severe setbacks. Some agricultural products from the Philippines in demand in Japan like cotton were now planted by Japanese planters.

The land held by the *mestizos* became idle throughout the Japanese occupation. Due to scarce supply, prices of goods skyrocketed. However, after the formal surrender of Japan to the American-led Allied Forces in August 1945, trade and investment gains again shifted to American markets and interests.

Post-Independence Administrations (1946–1964)

On 4 July 1946, in accordance with the provisions of the Tydings-McDuffie Law, the Philippines was granted independence by the United States. Filipino administrators found themselves faced with economic responsibilities far greater than they had envisioned. The war left the country with severe economic instability and physical destruction. Within months after the declaration of independence, it requested development assistance from the United States.

Despite gaining independence, the Philippines remained closely linked to the United States politically, economically and culturally. Successive Philippine administrations and the policies they formulated and implemented clearly showed a bias towards doing business with the United States. For instance, parity rights in the 1935 Constitution and the Bell Trade Act continued to give US businesses equal rights to exploit the natural resources and operate public utilities in exchange for special preferential treatment for Philippine exports to the United States. In 1947, President Manuel Roxas signed the Military Bases Agreement, which gave the United States extra-territorial rights over their armed forces installations in the Philippines for the next 99 years.

In the post-independence period, officials from the two countries signed the Laurel-Langley Agreement, which became the basis for special bilateral trade relations between the countries. In terms of security, President Carlos Garcia signed the Bohlen-Serrano Agreement in 1959, thereby shortening the 99-year lease of the American military installations in the Philippines to 25 years.

Past and Present Philippine Presidents

Emilio F. Aguinaldo (1898–1901), First President of the First Philippine Republic

Manuel L. Quezon (1935–1944), First President of the Philippine Commonwealth

Sergio S. Osmena, Sr. (1944–1946), Second President of the Philippine Commonwealth

Jose P. Laurel (1943–1945), President of the Occupied Philippine Republic

Manuel A. Roxas (1946–1948), Last President of the Philippine Commonwealth and the First President of the Third Philippine Republic

Elpidio R. Quirino (1948–1953), Second President of the Third Philippine Republic

Ramon F. Magsaysay (1953–1957), Third President of the Third Philippine Republic

Carlos P. Garcia (1957–1961), Fourth President of the Third Philippine Republic

Diosdado P. Macapagal (1961–1965), Fifth President of the Third Philippine Republic

Ferdinand E. Marcos (1965–1986), Sixth President of the Third Philippine Republic

Corazon C. Aquino (1985–1992), Seventh President of the Third Philippine Republic

Fidel V. Ramos (1992–present), Eighth President of the Third Philippine Republic

---

Marcos and Martial Law (1965–1986)

On 21 September 1972, President Ferdinand E. Marcos, using emergency powers granted to him as chief executive by the 1935 Constitution, declared martial law in the Philippines. Under a national state of emergency, Marcos successfully extended his term of office beyond the constitutional term limit, which would expire in 1973. He set himself up for a better deal with an unlimited stay in office. He further "legalised" his actions by coercing members of 26,000 citizen assemblies he created to approve a new constitution that gave him almost unrestricted authority.

Marcos effectively consolidated massive power in one person—himself. The implementation of Article 17 of the Constitution meant that the executive branch would be left unchecked by an elected legislature. Meanwhile, members of the judicial branch remained passive throughout the whole time for fear of being jailed. Judges were left with no choice but to be supportive of the massive arrests and detention without trial, which were carried out with the suspension of the writ of *habeas corpus*. No separation of powers existed that would give each branch the ability to check and balance the other. With the two branches "knocked out" and the armed forces as a "new branch", the stage was set for Marcos' so-called New Society programme.

With the imposition of martial law, Marcos swiftly moved to accomplish the many political and administrative tasks he considered necessary for the smooth operation of his New Society programme. Firstly, he abolished the Philippine Congress and arrested senators and congressmen who opposed him on charges of being communist "destabilisers". Secondly, he mandated that all civil service employees submit themselves to an Integrated Reorganisation Plan—disloyal employees were thus purged. Thirdly, he requested judges at all levels of the court system to submit their courtesy resignations. Fourthly, he issued "much-needed" presidential decrees, letters of instructions, general directives and executive orders, cracking down on militant labour groups, and student organisations. Finally, he confiscated and nationalised private power, water and other vital industries owned by his opponents.

Marcos did all this in the name of safeguarding the country's economic interests and maintaining its political stability. After successfully launching this first phase of dictatorial rule, he proceeded to institutionalise a state-oriented development strategy by setting up a centralised politico-administrative structure, providing special economic perks and incentives to loyal friends and relatives, expanding the public enterprise sector, and marginalising many segments of civil society.

Significant Events in Philippine History

1414	Chinese merchant vessel sinks off the coast of Palawan
1521	Ferdinand Magellan sets foot on Philippine soil
1896	Jose Rizal is executed at the Luneta
1898	Independence from Spain and the start of American occupation
1942–1945	Japanese occupation
1946	Independence from the United States
1947	US Military Bases Agreement
1967	The Philippines, along with five neighbouring countries, form ASEAN
1972	Ferdinand Marcos declares martial law
1986	People power revolution topples Marcos
1991	US Military forced to withdraw
1992	Fidel Ramos succeeds Corazon Aquino

Redemocratisation and Market Liberalisation (1986–Present)

The post-Marcos years saw many political and economic developments, which restored democracy and liberalised the market. Despite continuing challenges, the Philippines seems to be headed towards NIC status by the year 2000.

Reestablishing Democratic Institutions

Marcos, the cronies he pampered and the state-oriented development regime they concocted caused severe socio-economic problems. From a growth rate second to Japan in the Asian region in the mid-1960s, the country's economy declined and eventually settled at the bottom by the 1980s. A "people power revolution" in February 1986 toppled Marcos. This uprising was led by Corazon Cojuangco Aquino, the widow of Marcos' political nemesis, Benigno Aquino. Critical support was provided by Armed Forces Vice Chief-of-Staff, General Fidel V. Ramos and Marcos' long-time Defence Minister Juan Ponce Enrile. Not surprisingly, mass-based support came from many of the groups that Marcos marginalised under his state-oriented regime. However, in retrospect, the term "revolution" is a misnomer as the events of February 1986 simply replaced one set of elites with another—a political change but not necessarily a social one.

Benigno Aquino once said, "Whoever comes after Marcos will have one heck of a time", not knowing his wife would be the one. By the time Corazon Aquino took over the reins of government, the country faced many major challenges. For instance, there was the debt-ridden economy with foreign borrowings mostly owed by an inefficient and ineffective public enterprise sector. The Philippines also had a number of protectionist trade barriers and an investment regime that favoured only a few Marcos cronies and turned away many foreign investors. The situation was not helped by a bloated and corruption-infested administrative system. What was more, the country had a socio-politically distressed population, with 80% living below the poverty line and many societal groups marginalised.

The Aquino administration began with the restoration of democratic institutions—an elected Congress and a people-ratified Constitution in 1987. With a legislature dominated by the ruling party, the task of enacting laws that would revive the economy became one of the government's main priorities. This started with a law to devolve power to the country's numerous local government units (LGUs) with the passage of the Local Government Code in 1991 (Republic Act 7160). Under Kalakalan 20 (Republic Act 6810), countryside businesses, as well as local small and medium enterprises (SMEs) were encouraged with perks, such as exemptions from national and local taxes, and licence and building permits within five years of their registration as countryside business enterprises (CBEs). To complement this law was the passage of the Cooperative Code of the Philippines (Republic Act 6938), which promoted the organisation and development of economic, credit and financial cooperatives.

Reinventing the whole trade and investment regime was a massive task that needed the active support of the duly elected senators and representatives in Congress. The legislators responded positively by passing laws that deregulated the banking, telecommunications, shipping and airline industries. In the banking sector, foreign banks were granted permission to operate branches in the Philippines. These banks were also allowed to buy into existing local banks. The Foreign Investments Act of 1991 (Republic Act 7042) simplified the entry requirements for foreign investors and provided for greater foreign equity participation in investment ventures.

Import liberalisation measures removed many quantitative restrictions on critical factors related to production. Additionally, tariffs were reduced for raw materials, intermediate goods and capital equipment.

Foreign exchange regulation was also significantly relaxed with the lifting of a 40-year-old restriction on virtually all international currency transactions.

Another growth-inducing bill passed in Congress during Aquino's administration was the Build-Operate-Transfer Law (Republic Act 6957), which authorised private sector participation in the financing, construction, operation and maintenance of much-needed infrastructure.

However, a number of failed military coups as well as the continuing Muslim and communist insurgencies gave prospective foreign and local investors the impression that the country was still politically volatile, a situation which was reflected in the country's dismal economic performance until Aquino's departure. This was despite the restoration of democratic institutions during her rule. Filipinos have now grown impatient, not realising that dismantling an ineffective economic set-up that took more than 20 years to institutionalise cannot be done overnight.

Pushing Through Economic Reforms

In 1992, Fidel V. Ramos, Aquino's anointed successor, became the eighth president of the Philippines. President Ramos quickly built upon the foundation laid down by the Aquino administration by pushing strongly for the implementation of market-based economic reforms.

Using the economic reform policies and programmes initiated during the Aquino administration, he pushed through the privatisation of government-owned and controlled corporations. He facilitated the implementation of the Build-Operate-Transfer Law, which encouraged public-private partnerships, especially in the infrastructure and energy sectors.

By 1993, the market-enhancing reforms gave the Philippines refreshing dividends. Thereafter, even as natural calamities and man-made crises continued to test its mettle, the country's economy surged to register positive real Gross National Product (GNP) growth rates for a fourth consecutive year, from 5.4% in 1995 to a remarkable 7.1% before the end of 1996. Moreover, inflation was brought down to a single digit in this period.

The country also registered a fiscal surplus for the third straight year. One of the results of these economic reform policies was a business-friendly environment that attracted numerous local and foreign investors to the Philippines.

With policy guidance from the administration, merchandise exports and investment—the two fastest growing sectors of the economy—posted impressive 15.4% and 13.7% gains respectively. Foreign direct investments also increased significantly. Some positive economic highlights were a decline in interest rates, high savings and investment rates, improved tax collection, and a stable peso. Moreover, during the last three years, the country experienced government budget surpluses after two decades of persistent national accounts deficits.

PAL: Getting More Competitive through Privatisation and Modernisation

Philippine Airlines (PAL), with its 56-year history, is one of the country's most enduring companies. It, in fact, was Asia's first airline. Due to the government's recent privatisation efforts and deregularisation initiatives, PAL's management launched an ambitious US$4 billion modernisation programme that involved the acquisition of 36 brand-new aircraft from Boeing (USA) and Airbus Industrie (France).

With the new aircraft purchases, PAL will have a fleet age of three-and-a-half years, which will make it one of the youngest fleets in the world. It will have the distinction of being the first airline in the world to operate all three of Airbus' new-generation type aircraft—the ultra-long A340 series 300 and series 200; the twin-engine, medium-to-long range A330 series 300; and the single-aisle A320. These aircraft are described by aviation industry watchers as some of the most efficient in the world.

PAL continues to invest valuable resources into maintenance operations, systems computerisation, personnel training and client satisfaction. With over 120 departures from Manila and Cebu to more than 19 points across the Asia-Pacific region, the PAL network is one of the busiest in the Far East.

The airline industry benefited from Ramos' economic liberalisation policies. Capitalising on the deregulation of domestic aviation, several small ambitious airlines have sprung up to serve parts of the country that were largely isolated only a few years ago. PAL has even shown interest in becoming an international carrier, a feat now possible through increased private sector participation and relaxed currency exchange controls.

As Trade Secretary Cesar Bautista recently pointed out, the Philippines is "way behind where it deserves to be—the result of years of neglect, complacency and wastages both in terms of government and business policies, mindset and activities". But he also stressed that current technology offers exciting new opportunities to move forward at a faster pace, to catch up and surge ahead. He called it "leapfrogging to prosperity"—an apt description of an economy creating thousands of new jobs and opening its markets to products from around the world.

CHAPTER 3

Government and Politics for the Business Person

Doing business in the Philippines does not refer only to transactions with members of the private sector. In the course of setting up and maintaining a business, a business person inevitably deals with national and sub-national government agencies They include customs agents in air and sea ports, tax collectors from the Bureau of Internal Revenue (BIR), and clerical officers in permit and licensing counters at the local municipality or at the Department of Trade and Industry (DTI) office, where you will be establishing your business operations.

The performance of politicians and government officials is a favourite topic for discussion in the Philippines. Assisted by the aggressive Philippine press, considered one of the most liberal in Asia, headline news are sometimes sensationalised issues.

The Philippine Government, like any other in the world, is a potential client for a wide range of goods and services, from paper clips to bridge construction. One of these business areas might just be your company's cup of tea. Hence, it is imperative for the business person to have a basic grasp of the workings of the Philippine Government and politics to boost his or her formal business interactions as well as gain an invaluable insight into informal dealings with clients and colleagues. After all, Philippine bureaucrats and politicians are not just power brokers but are also important deal makers.

Philippine Government

The Philippines is a democratic and republican state where civilian authority is, at all times, supreme over the military. The fundamental law is the 1987 Constitution of the Philippines. Basically, the national government set-up is similar to the US system and is divided into three major branches—the executive, legislative and judicial. Each branch is independent of the other.

Theoretically, there is a separation of powers arrangement that allows one branch to act as a check-and-balance for the other. In reality, members of all three branches know that communication, coordination and cooperation are crucial for the smooth passage and implementation of any public policy on business or other issues.

Executive Branch

This branch of the Philippine Government is headed by an elected president who serves a single six-year term of office. Civilian authority is always supreme; hence the president is also the commander-in-chief of the armed forces.

Elected at the same time as the president is the vice-president, who also serves a six-year term but can be re-elected for another successive term. The president and vice-president must be natural-born citizens of the Philippines, at least 40 years old, literate, registered voters and residents for not less than 10 years immediately preceding the day of the election. The president is succeeded by the vice-president upon the death, removal from office, resignation or permanent disability of the former.

Assisting the president are cabinet members who are appointed by him or her (with the concurrence of the Appointment Committee in Congress) to head various governmental departments, including regulatory agencies. They hold the official title of secretary. Included in the cabinet are heads of presidential commission and committees, as well as presidential advisers. The president has the power to declare martial rule only with the concurrence of the legislature.

The official residence and office of the president is Malacanang Palace along the Pasig River in San Miguel, Manila.

Members of the President's Cabinet

Vice-President
Executive Secretary
Agrarian Reform Secretary
Agriculture Secretary
Budget and Management Secretary
Commission on Higher Education Chairman
Council of Economic Advisers to the President
Education, Culture and Sports Secretary
Energy Secretary
Environment and Natural Resources Secretary
Finance Secretary
Foreign Affairs Secretary
Health Secretary
Interior and Local Government Secretary
Justice Secretary
Labour and Employment Secretary
Metro Manila Development Authority Chairman
National Defence Secretary
National Economic and Development
Authority Director-General
Public Works and Highways Secretary
Science and Technology Secretary
Social Welfare and Development Secretary
Tourism Secretary
Trade and Industry Secretary
Transportation and Communications Secretary
Presidential Adviser on Countryside Development
Presidential Adviser for Housing and HUDCC Chairman
Presidential Adviser on the Peace Process
Presidential Adviser for Youth Affairs
Presidential Legal Counsel
Presidential Legislative Adviser
Presidential Security Adviser
Director General, National Security Council
Press Secretary

The Aquino and Ramos administrations launched an aggressive privatisation programme, which targeted many state-owned enterprises. However, the government still maintains a number of critical government-owned or controlled corporations (GOCCs) attached to line agencies in the executive branch. Most of the remaining GOCCs are in areas considered part of the national patrimony. The government still has a strong presence in the transportation, power, financial, and agricultural and tourism sectors. However, with the passage of the privatisation law and the encouragement of public-private partnerships, its share of the economy through the GOCCs has declined.

Public officials, from secretaries to directors, are formally addressed by their titles, for example, "Under-secretary", followed by their name.

Need Investment Matchmaking Advice and Assistance?

When in need of export marketing support, investors may consult the following executive branch agencies for free assistance (full particulars are in appendix B):

Export Assistance Network (Exponet): Provides matchmaking services between exporters and buyers/raw materials suppliers

Bureau of Export Trade Promotion (BETP): Provides market information, strategy, product research and foreign trade assistance

Garment and Textile Export Board One Stop Action Centre: Gives garments export assistance

Philippine International Trading Corporation (PITC): Provides help on trading with socialist and transitional economies

Centre for International Trade Expositions and Missions (CITEM): Provides assistance on trade fairs/exhibitions

Product Development and Design Centre for the Philippines (PDDCP): Provides assistance on product development and improvement

National Subcontractors Exchange (Subconex): Provides subcontracting facilitation between contractors and subcontractors.

Legislative Branch

Lawmaking power is vested in the Philippine Congress, which consists of the Senate (upper house) and the House of Representatives (lower house). There are 24 senators, all of whom are elected by the country's qualified voters. The term of office of each senator is six years. He or she is only allowed to serve two consecutive terms. According to the 1987 Constitution, a person qualifies to be an elected senator if he or she is a natural-born citizen of the Philippines, at least 35 years old, literate, a registered voter and resident of the country for not less than two years immediately preceding the day of the election.

The most powerful person in the Senate is the Senate President. He or she presides over each session of the Senate. Senators sponsor or author bills or resolutions on important matters, such as business regulation and agrarian reforms. When meeting a senator, it is best to address the person by his or her title. Formal written communications should have the word "Honourable" or "Hon." in front of their names.

The House of Representatives consists of not more than 200 members, representing legislative districts apportioned among the provinces, cities and Metropolitan Manila area based on the population distribution. Members of the lower legislative chamber are called representatives or congressmen. Some representatives are appointed by the president to represent the youths, overseas Filipinos and indigenous communities. A congressman's term of office is three years and limited to three consecutive terms.

A person is qualified to run as a representative if he or she is a natural-born citizen of the Philippines, at least 25 years old, literate, a registered voter and resident of the country for not less than one year immediately preceding the day of the election. Congressmen sponsor or author bills or resolutions on important matters, such as trade and investment, and rural development. The House of Representatives is headed by the House Speaker. Each bill must pass through three readings in the upper and lower houses of the

President Fidel V. Ramos, the eighth president of the Third Philippine Republic. He has introduced many measures to help the economy since taking office.

Philippine Congress. Both legislative chambers must reconcile similar bills in a conference committee, sometimes referred to as the "third house".

Finally, the bill must be signed into law by the Philippine President. One of the most important bills passed by the Congress is the yearly national budget or the Annual Appropriations Act, which is sponsored by the chairman of the Senate Finance Committee. Aside from investor-friendly legislation, such as the Foreign Investments Act of 1991 (Republic Act 7042) and the Build-Operate-Transfer Law (Republic Act 6957), the executive and legislative branches have joined forces to formulate and execute laws on labour and wage rationalisation (Republic Act 6727), comprehensive agrarian reform (Republic Act 6657), social housing (Republic Act 6846), and the maintenance of peace and order (Republic Act 6975), among others.

Judicial decisions and pronouncements, letters of instructions, presidential decrees, administrative orders, and rules and regulations issued can come from any of the three branches of government to become the law of the land.

Judicial Branch

The powers of the executive and legislative branches of the Philippine Government are checked by the judicial branch. The Supreme Court consists of a chief justice and 14 associate justices. Members of the Supreme Court and judges of lower courts are appointed by the president from a list of nominees prepared by the judicial and bar council, which is chaired by the chief justice of the Supreme Court. Presidential appointments to the courts do not need congressional approval.

No person can be appointed member of the Supreme Court or any lower collegiate courts unless he or she is a natural-born citizen of the Philippines. To qualify for appointment to the Supreme Court, one must also be 40 years of age, and must have been a judge for 15 years or more in the lower courts or engaged in the practice of law in the Philippines. The Supreme Court has the final judgement on the validity or constitutionality of any treaty, executive agreement, law, presidential decree, proclamation, order, and other presidential issuances.

According to the 1987 Constitution, administrative supervision over all courts and their personnel is vested in the Supreme Court. Philippine law contains a mixture of Spanish law, Anglo-American law, Roman law and the indigenous customs and traditions of the Filipino people. Major sources of jurisprudence include the Penal Code, Civil Code, Labour Code and the Code of Commerce. Judicial officials are formally addressed as "Justice" or "Judge", followed by their name.

Constitutional Commissions

The Philippines also has three independent constitutional bodies. These are the Civil Service Commission (CSC), Commission on Elections (COMELEC) and the Commission on Audit (COA). All three enjoy relative fiscal and personnel autonomy. Members of these commissions do not hold any other office or employment during his or her tenure. The Civil Service Commission has three members, the Commission on Elections has seven, while the Commission on Audit has three, all appointed by the president for fixed terms of office.

The primary task of the Civil Service Commission is to ensure that all appointments to public service are made according to merit and fitness. A major role of the Commission on Elections is to enforce and administer all laws and regulations pertaining to the conduct of fair and free elections, plebiscites, initiatives, referenda and recalls. The main objective of the Commission on Audit is to examine, audit and settle all accounts relating to the revenues and expenditures of all Philippine Government agencies, including government-owned or controlled corporations. The proper title for members of these commissions is "Commissioner", followed by their name.

Local Government Units

There are 77 provinces, 67 cities, 1,540 municipalities and 41,927 *barangays* (village communities) in the Philippines. Under the Local Government Code passed in 1991 (Republic Act 7160), many administrative and financial functions handled by the national government are now devolved to these Local Government Units (LGUs). This means that a larger share of revenues from taxes collected at the national level are being shared with LGUs.

LGUs are also given the authority to impose local taxes and fees, as well as provide perks and incentives (such as tax breaks or fee waivers) to businesses wishing to set up operations in their geographic area of responsibility. The Local Government Code provides guidelines for the creation of consultative and deliberative fora like school boards, health boards, development councils, and peace and order councils to facilitate socio-economic development at the local level. This includes creating an atmosphere that is trade and investment-friendly. LGUs are now competing against one another for local and foreign business, resulting in a host of perks and incentive packages for investors.

Development Responsibilities of LGUs

At the Provincial Level
- Provide agricultural, industrial and research services
- Enforce forestry laws with the government's help
- Provide healthcare and other tertiary services
- Offer welfare services, including relief programmes
- Build and maintain public buildings, jails, parks and other facilities
- Build and maintain roads, bridges, waterworks, drainage and irrigation
- Implement programmes for low-cost housing
- Offer investment support services like credit financing
- Upgrade and modernise tax information and collection
- Provide inter-municipal telecommunications services
- Implement tourism development and promotion projects

At the Municipality Level
- Provide research services for agro-industries
- Implement community-based forestry projects
- Implement healthcare programmes
- Provide social welfare services
- Provide information on investment and job placement
- Develop a solid waste disposal as well as an environmental management system
- Build and maintain municipal buildings, parks, roads, schools and ports

At the City Level
- Provide all the services of a municipality and province
- Provide communication and transportation facilities
- Give support to education, police and fire services

At the Barangay Level
- Provide agricultural, health and welfare services
- Administer the *barangay* court
- Maintain roads, water supply and other infrastructure
- Disseminate information and provide reading centres

The Armed Forces of the Philippines

Although the president is the commander-in-chief of the Armed Forces of the Philippines (AFP), the military establishment has been likened by many political scientists to a formidable fourth branch of the Philippine Government.

The primary purpose of the armed services bureaucracy, comprising the army, navy and the air force, is to maintain internal security and external defence. Although battle-tested both within and outside the country, the AFP lacks the modern equipment of military services present in neighbouring countries.

However, under the AFP Modernisation Plan, its external defence capability has been beefed up with purchases of more modern weapons systems, naval vessels and tactical aircraft.

In times of peace, the AFP is an active partner in the nation's countryside development programmes. Military servicemen and civilian personnel also help build and maintain roads, bridges, schools, playgrounds, as well as provide assistance and coordination in times of disaster.

The external defence of the country was, for a long time, heavily subsidised by the United States Armed Forces under the Military Bases Agreement (MBA). This changed in 1991 when the Philippine Senate rejected a new MBA, which forced the US military to withdraw its facilities from the Philippines. Despite the US departure, the Mutual Defence Treaty of 1951 continues to be the legal basis for on-going joint military exercises between the Philippines and the United States armed services as part of their regional alliance network. Moreover, the US navy makes port visits to the Philippines under a Continued Access Agreement (CAA) signed before the closure of the American installations. US warships are still frequent visitors to their former berths in Subic Bay. These security arrangements maintained by the US military assure nations in the Southeast Asian region that critical sea lanes in the South China Seas and Pacific Ocean remain free from unfriendly obstructions.

Apart from traditional duties, many in the armed forces have taken on non-traditional roles and become government officials and elected lawmakers. Politicised during the martial law years, many generals and admirals become high-ranking public servants after they retire from active service. Some former military officers also run for elections and become mayors, governors, representatives, and senators. One West Point-trained general even went on become the president!

Constitutions (1935, 1973 & 1987)
The first fundamental law of the Philippines, the 1935 Constitution, reflected the ideals of both the liberal democracy and market-based capitalism of the United States. After all, it was adopted by Filipinos while the country was still a US Commonwealth. The 1935 Constitution helped preserve preferential treatment to US goods and services in the Philippines.

Even after the country gained independence in 1945, the US Government felt secure as American landholding and other vital business interests in the former colony were protected by law. One of Marcos' promises, which won him two terms as president, was to change this biased scenario and make the country's economy more "pro-Filipino".

The 1973 Constitution, popularly known as the Marcos Constitution, was a basic law passed under Marcos' martial law and approved by the electorate through his "peoples' assemblies". It eliminated many of the pro-US provisions. However, Marcos replaced them with sections that virtually gave him dictatorial powers. He then used these powers to transform the economy into one that was dominated by his anointed capitalist cronies.

After Marcos was ousted in 1986, his successor Corazon Aquino immediately convened a Constitutional Commission (Concom), which drafted a fundamental law that basically sought to re-democratise the country and make it a more business-friendly place. It was passed in 1987 and continues to be the basis for the

Philippines' thriving political democracy and market-based trade and investment regime. It contains many provisions, like social justice and human rights, which are reactions to the excesses of the Marcos regime.

Philippine Politics for the Business Person

There are instances when knowing the proper application procedures or regulatory process might not be enough for doing business in the Philippines. Wading through the Philippine Governmental morass can be quite time-consuming (and intimidating), especially for a newcomer. To cut down on time-wasting government transactions costs, it might be wise to have connections either inside or outside the government organisation concerned. Bribes and other corrupt means may work in the short-term but the wise business person must think in terms of the long-term. Your strategic plans for the Philippines should include not only building a solid client base but also a good network of government connections.

How can these important government networks be nurtured in the Philippine context? This is where your working knowledge of the bureaucracy, dovetailed with a grasp of domestic politics, come in handy. Keep in mind that most Philippine bureaucrats are beholden to politicians. Politicians or people well-connected to them, whether in the metropolitan areas or in the provinces, are the business person's best bet when in need of expeditious public transactions. Nobody knows the ins and outs of the Philippine Government better than a Filipino who works (or used to work) as a high-ranking civil servant or politicians who have official business interactions with these public officers.

Filipinos in politics have informal arrangements and agreements with key civil servants developed over generations. Inviting high-ranking politicians and public administrators to your company's social events (for example, Christmas parties, new branch or factory openings and anniversaries) is a good approach.

In some cases, "entertainment" expenses may be incurred. Rest assured that the net result will be worth it. This practice is culturally acceptable. You will also make more friends in the process.

Clans and Dynasties

The previous chapter highlighted the Chinese and Spanish *mestizos* as elites who dominated the political, economic and social landscape of the Philippines. Over the years, many of the rich families became integral parts of larger clans. Intermarriages among created an even more complex web of inter-relationships. Due to their wealth and power, some families were able to extend their influence in local and national politics for generations by forming political and economic dynasties.

A large part (more than 70%) of the Philippine economy is still controlled by only 20% of the population. There are Filipino-Chinese clans who control a large segment of the lucrative retail and wholesale sectors. For instance, the Tys own Metrobank, the Sys own Shoemart, the Gokongweis own Robinsons, Manila Times and Robina Farms, and the Tans own Fortune Tobacco, Allied Bank, Asia Brewery and control Philippine Airlines. Aside from megamalls, Filipino-Chinese families are into real estate, banking, shipping, agriculture, mining and other industries.

Not to be outdone are the Filipino-Spanish *mestizo* clans like the Zobels, Ayalas and Sorianos who control established companies like Ayala Corporation and San Miguel Corporation. There are also the traditionally landed families like the Lopezes, Aranetas, Yulos and Osmenas who are now into diversified business interests. Although mostly supportive of one another, there are times when family feuds occur. The saying "blood is thicker than water but business is business" is true in these instances.

Ethnicity and Regionalism

Filipinos come from a mix of 110 linguistic, cultural and racial groupings. These wide-ranging ethnic backgrounds are represented

Muslims make up just one of the many religious groupings in the culturally diverse but predominantly Catholic country.

in various aspects of Philippine politics. There are more than 70 dialects and 11 native languages spoken in the country's 77 provinces spread across more than 7,100 islands. There are also different types of *mestizos* (mixed ethnicity) who have been ethnically influenced by people from Europe, America, and other parts of Asia like China and India.

Generally, people from the Philippines call themselves Filipinos. Most will lay claim to their ethnic background, which is based on linguistic differences or province of origin. So do not be puzzled when Filipinos also call themselves Cebuano, Ilocano, Kapampangan or Tausog. *Mestizos* will sometimes distinguish themselves as Filipino-Chinese or *Tisoy* (a Spanish *mestizo*).

Aside from ethnic loyalties, a business person should keep in mind that in the Philippines, the 77 provinces, including Metropolitan Manila and its outlying areas, are clustered into 15 regional sub-groupings. Regional loyalties, like ethnic loyalties are therefore common. For administrative purposes, each national government department has regional offices based on these sub-groupings. Provincial leaders in one region may at times band together to form lobbying blocks pushing for legislation favourable to their area. Sometimes, these leaders just want a larger portion of the "pork barrel" for their administrative region.

Regional Divisions in the Philippines

Name	Area Covered	Number of Provinces
NCR	National Capital Region	Metro Manila
ARMM	Autonomous Region of Muslim Mindanao	4
CAR	Cordillera Administrative Region	5
Region 1	Ilocos	4
Region 2	Cagayan Valley	5
Region 3	Central Luzon	6
Region 4	Southern Tagalog	11
Region 5	Bicol	6
Region 6	Western Visayas	6
Region 7	Central Visayas	4
Region 8	Eastern Visayas	6
Region 9	Western Mindanao	3
Region 10	Northeastern Mindanao	7
Region 11	Southeastern Mindanao	6
Region 12	Central Mindanao	3

Technocrats and Cronies

Every Filipino President has a group of friends and colleagues who pledge loyalty to him or her. They are popularly known as his or her technocrats and cronies. Each member of this close circle of advisers has a role to play in either formulating or implementing policies. This political phenomena of having technocrats and cronies occurs not just at the national level—most local government leaders are also surrounded by them.

The terms, technocrats and cronies, became popular during the Marcos years. The two labels were used interchangeably to describe the private sector oligarchy he developed, made up of loyal relatives and friends. Marcos used his cronies and technocrats as a counterweight against the wealth and power of the traditional elite families like the Lopezes and Osmenias.

The grand coalition of elites was notoriously known as Marcos cronies. They included Disini, Cuenca, Silverio, Benedicto, Floriendo, Cojuangco and others. Marcos recruited these key allies from the First Family's former classmates, friends and relatives, fraternity brothers, golf buddies, and province mates. His legion of cronies also included many high-ranking military officials who played a key role in maintaining discipline and obedience during his martial law regime. Many also became beneficiaries of economic handouts and lucrative political positions even before retiring from the armed forces. Nowadays the label, cronies or technocrats, is used simply to describe people who take advantage of their access to power to gain special favours, perks and benefits from the government.

Connections to a crony or technocrat may be useful to a company that needs insider information on policy discussions or tips on bid specifications. The unpredictable nature of Philippine politics may affect valuable connections, so it is a common strategy among local business people not to place all their loyalties in one technocrat or crony. Diversification is the key.

Political Parties and Interest Groups

Although the governmental set-up is based on the US system, the political party system is no longer so. What began as a loose two-party system evolved into the vibrant multi-party system that it is today. A broad spectrum of ideological leanings are represented, from leftists and centrists to rightists. Marcos tried to establish a dominant one-party system under martial law with the founding of the Kilusang Bagong Lipunan (KBL).

Nowadays, rainbow coalitions are common because of the sheer number of parties and the need to pool together resources and eventually, votes. For instance, the Lakas (Corazon Aquino's Party), the National Union of Christian Democrats (NUCD) and the United Muslim Democrats of the Philippines (UMDP) formed a coalition that supported Ramos' bid for presidency in 1992. Party machinery is important in terms of mobilising mass support. Established parties' influence extends to the grassroots.

Similarly, a large number of interest groups (also sometimes referred to as NGOs or Non-governmental Organisations) abound in the Philippines. They advocate such issues concerning land reform, labour, women, the environment, education and religion. Like political parties, some of these interest groups can be either highly conservative or militant.

Even after the EDSA "people power" revolution, it is still commonplace to see various interest groups holding rallies and vigils, setting up pickets and going on marches. Aided by the country's free press, they can mount effective lobbies against bureaucrats and politicians. However, these interest groups are also sometimes viewed as a major source of traffic jams, especially when they hold protests on or along major streets and highways.

Church and Politics

The Philippines is the only predominantly Christian country in Asia. About 83% of the population are Roman Catholics. The remainder belong to the other religious faiths. There are two highly visible independent churches in the country, the Inglesia ni Cristo (Church of Christ) and the Aglipay (Philippine Independent Church).

A foreigner in the Philippines who goes to a Catholic church for the first time would most likely conclude that "separation of church and state" does not exist in the country. Whether in Metro Manila or the provinces, newcomers have to get used to homilies, sermons and pastoral letters that deal with controversial political issues and political personalities. Church leaders feel that it is their duty to comment and criticise errant policies and erring politicians. It is interesting to note that the name of the highest-ranking Catholic clergyman is Jaime Cardinal Sin.

There are also religious groups that strongly influence voting patterns, especially the El Shaddai. Some of these religious groups are led by charismatic individuals.

Electoral Contests

Some Filipinos are born into political families and are, therefore, destined to become politicians. However, this does not mean that the rest of the population of the Philippines are just passive actors in the political arena.

Frequency of Elections

Presidential	Every six years
Senators	Every six years
Representatives	Every three years
Governors, Mayors and Councils	Every three years
Barangays	Every three years

Most Filipinos, especially the so-called masses, look forward to electoral contests. It is a time to show their loyalty (or disloyalty) to their political patrons. Electoral contests are very much personality-based instead of issue-oriented, although the latter is slowly becoming a strong determinant of victory. Television personalities also have a good chance of being elected because of their high recognition factor. Classic examples are: Vice-President Joseph Estrada and Senator Ramon Rerilla. Being married to an actor or actress may also help a politician's cause.

However, a certain segment of the population, depending on regional loyalties, continues to back "brand" names like the Laurels, Macapagals, Osmenas, Cuencos, Marcoses and Rectos. For instance, despite their notoriety, the Marcoses and Romualdezes are still the political family to beat in their Ilocos Norte and Leyte strongholds.

CHAPTER 4

Getting Your Business Started

The Philippines' liberalised business environment has made the country attractive to both local and foreign investors. It has an administration committed to economic and trade reform, a generally positive attitude towards foreign investment, a highly trainable English-speaking workforce, and emerging economic zones that make the country an attractive base for manufacturing export products. This chapter outlines the regulatory framework for doing business in the Philippines. It provides information about policies and procedures for organising the business enterprise, investment procedures and requirements, foreign trade policies, banking and foreign exchange policies, taxation, human resources and industrial relations, environmental regulations, protection of investment and intellectual property, and acquisition of real estate.

Organising the Business Enterprise

Business Organisations with Foreign Participation

The main types of business organisations in the Philippines are sole proprietorship, partnerships and corporations. The most popular business type is the share corporation with a charter limited to 50 years that is renewable for succeeding 50-year terms. Other less common business types include joint stock companies, joint accounts, business trusts and cooperatives.

A foreign firm may also operate in the Philippines through a branch. In addition, foreign firms may also establish and register a subsidiary, a licensing or franchising agreement, a foreign-Filipino joint venture agreement or a regional headquarters. The Philippines' Securities and Exchange Commission (SEC) monitors the registration of partnerships and corporations. The SEC has absolute jurisdiction and control over all corporations, partnerships and associations.

Representative Offices   Representative or liaison offices of foreign companies deal with the clients of the parent company but do not derive income from the Philippines. They are subsidised by the head office. They undertake information dissemination, promotion of the company's products and other such non-income-generating activities. Representative offices must be registered with the SEC.

Branches   Considered simple extensions of the parent company, branches need to be registered with the SEC. After obtaining a licence, a branch must deposit cash or government securities equivalent to PHP100,000 (about US$3,000) and 2% of gross income in excess of PHP5 million (about US$145,000) each fiscal year thereafter.[1] Branch offices are allowed to conduct all types of business operations that are approved by the Board of Investments (BOI), including marketing, rendering of services, processing or assembling of semi-finished products, manufacturing and licensing.

Subsidiaries   A subsidiary is a separate entity that is distinct from the parent company. If the parent company holds more than 40% of the equity of the subsidiary, the subsidiary must register with the BOI if it wishes to utilise certain incentives provided under the Philippine law and must, in any event, register as a domestic corporation with the SEC. Parent companies may control a subsidiary through the establishment of devices, such as proxies and voting trust agreements. As the subsidiary is a separate entity, the parent company is effectively insulated from subsidiary liabilities. A subsidiary is taxed on worldwide income.

Licensing/Franchise Agreements   These allow foreign firms to provide patents, trademarks, services, technology and other assets to Philippine companies in exchange for royalties. For royalties to be remitted in full (net of taxes), contracts for royalties or technical service contracts must be registered with the Bangko Sentral ng Pilipinas (BSP—the central bank). Royalty payments on copyrights (other than those for reprinting of textbooks and reference books) may be remitted in full, as may the royalties or fees on contracts and agreements not falling within the coverage of technology transfer agreements. One percent royalty is allowed on renewal agreements that involve the sole use of foreign trademarks.

Joint-venture Agreements Joint ventures are a common way for foreign firms to do business in the Philippines. The local partner typically contributes the hands-on market information and financial resources.

Regional Headquarters A regional headquarters acts as a supervisory authority over subsidiaries, branches and affiliates in the region outside the Philippines. It does not derive its income from its operations in the Philippines (and is not looked upon as actually having any business dealings in the Philippines). Multinational companies must remit to the Philippines a minimum amount annually to cover the operating expenses of their registered regional headquarters. In return, the companies enjoy liberalised resident visa privileges and limited income tax liability of 15% for foreigners. The regional office is also exempt from registration requirements with the municipal governments.

Establishing a Branch
Foreign corporations may obtain a certificate to do business through a branch or a resident agent by registering with the SEC. The SEC requires the following documents: a copy of the board resolution authorising the establishment of a branch office, a certificate of reciprocity, power of attorney designating a person

who is a resident of the Philippines, a statement of the corporation's solvency and sound financial standing, the latest annual report (financial statement, balance sheet and related statement of income and expenses), a copy of the articles of incorporation and bylaws (with an English translation, if necessary), and the completed information sheet, which is provided by the SEC along with the application forms.

Although branches and subsidiary corporations are subject to the same registration fees and the same requirements in regard to business licences and investment, their incomes are subject different taxes.

Companies licensed to do business locally but incorporated abroad, along with those operating as branches of foreign corporations, are required to deposit PHP100,000 in government bonds and equity instruments. Foreign firms receive interest and dividends on securities deposited with the SEC. When they cease operations, the securities are returned. Every fiscal year, such firms must put up additional deposits equivalent to 2% of all income over PHP5 million. These may be partly returned if income decreases or the actual market value of total securities on deposit increases by at least 10%.

Excluded from the deposit requirement are foreign banks (including offshore banking units), foreign insurance corporations, foreign non-share corporations, representative offices of foreign firms in the Philippines and the regional headquarters of multinationals. Most MNCs skirt this requirement by setting up distinctly incorporated companies in the Philippines, with relationships effected through technical-service agreements or technology licences.

In contrast, Japanese firms often set up branches in the Philippines, in which case the parent company is not dissociated from liabilities locally incurred by its Philippine branch.

Forming a Philippine Corporation

To form a corporation, the incorporators must subscribe to the proposed articles of incorporation and file documents (specifying the company name and purpose, principal office, capital distribution, and so forth) with the SEC. The treasurer must certify that at least 25% of the proposed capitalisation has been taken up and that 25% of the subscription has been paid up. The SEC requires foreigners to fully pay up the initial subscription at the time of incorporation. The incorporators then meet to elect a board of directors which in turn appoints the management.

The first step in SEC registration involves the SEC's Records Division checking the proposed corporate name for possible duplication. The verified name is still deemed unofficial until the issuance of the registration certificate. The next step is the approval of the articles of incorporation and the payment of corresponding fees. The applicant then submits three sets of required documents to the Records Division, which forwards the documents to the Examiners and Appraiser Department (for a review of the financial aspects of the incorporation) and the Corporate and Legal Department (for a review of the legal aspects). Upon recommendation, the supervising commissioner of the Corporate and Legal Department approves the certificate of registration, which is released through the Records Division. The process takes about a month. To facilitate registering new corporations, the SEC operates an "express lane", with application forms specially prepared for specific types of business. Filing normally takes one day, provided all necessary documents and prior clearances from other agencies are submitted in the morning.

Routine registrations are also required by other government agencies, such as the Bureau of Internal Revenue, the Bureau of Domestic Trade, the Department of Labour and Employment, the Social Security System, the Department of Finance, and the BSP. If the corporation is being organised either as a bank or as other financial intermediary, a certificate of authority from the central bank's monetary board is necessary. In general, the election of foreigners to the board of directors or governing body of a corporation or association engaged in partially restricted activities is permitted roughly in proportion to the permissible foreign participation or share of capital in such entities.

Investment Procedures and Requirements

Regulatory Framework

The Foreign Investments Act (FIA) of 1991 (Republic Act 7042, effective 1 July 1991) is more liberal than its predecessors.[2] It opened most enterprises to 100% foreign equity participation and simplified registration procedures for foreign investments. The FIA has a two-part "negative list" of areas where foreign investment is restricted.

The "A" list restricts foreign investment in certain areas due to legal and constitutional constraints. The areas include mass media, advertising, public utilities, most licensed professional services and the retail trade. The "B" list consists of activities regulated for reasons of security, defence, health and moral concerns, and protection of small and medium-scale enterprises. The FIA requires a minimum paid-up capital of US$200,000 for an enterprise to be more than 40% foreign-owned. The FIA's "C" list (activities deemed "adequately served" by existing enterprises) was abolished following the March 1996 amendments to the FIA.

Foreign investments in large high-profile projects, like power generation, industrial infrastructure and mineral exploitation may still attract local opposition. At least one project—the construction of a US$535 million cement factory by Taiwan's Tuntex Group in the northern province of Pangasinan—was denied clearance by the Department of Environment and Natural Resources in August 1996, following strong opposition from environmentalists and local residents. Several power projects have been delayed due to resistance from local communities.

The legal framework for foreign investments is the Foreign Investments Act of 1991 and the Omnibus Investments Code of 1987. These laws regulate the processes as well as the conditions under which non-Philippine nationals may invest and operate in the country.

Twelve General Business Start-up Requirements

1. **Registration of corporations and partnerships**: Securities and Exchange Commission (SEC)
2. **Registration of business name/single proprietorship**: Bureau of Trade Regulations and Consumer Protection (BTRCP)
3. **Registration for incentives under Executive Order 226**: Board of Investments (BOI)
4. **Registration of export firms** (for those wishing to locate in any of the country's export processing zones and availing themselves of incentives): Philippine Export Zone Authority (PEZA)
5. **Registration of foreign investments** (for the purpose of capital repatriation and profit remittances): Central Bank of the Philippines (CB)
6. **Tax Identification Number**: Bureau of Internal Revenue (BIR)
7. **Locational clearance/business permit** (for firms wishing to locate in Metro Manila): Metro Manila Authority (MMA)
8. **Building permit and licence to do business**: City Halls/ Municipal Offices in areas where the business will be set up
9. **Employer's Social Security (SS) number**: Social Security System
10. **Membership in the government health care benefits (GSIS) system**: MEDICARE
11. **Electrical services connection**: Manila Electric Co. (MERALCO) for businesses in the Meralco franchise area and local electric utility firms for those setting up business in non-MERALCO franchise areas
12. **Water services**: Metropolitan Waterworks and Sewerage System (MWSS) for firms wishing to locate in Metro Manila and Local Water Utilities Administration (LWUA) for those wishing to locate outside Metro Manila

Approval Process for Foreign Direct Investments

The BOI is the primary government entity dealing with foreign investments. It is advisable to formally register all foreign direct investments. The SEC registers, regulates, licenses and supervises all corporations and partnerships doing business in the Philippines. It also regulates the issuance and trading of securities.

The Bureau of Trade Regulations and Consumer Protection (BTRCP), an agency of the Department of Trade and Industry (DTI), has jurisdiction over the registration and regulation of a single proprietorship. Foreign exchange transactions, including the financing of imports and exports, are under the purview of the BSP and the Department of Finance. All inward transfers of foreign exchange for investment purposes must be registered to facilitate future profit remittances and capital repatriation.

Under the Foreign Investments Act, new foreign investments can be registered directly with the SEC (or the BTRCP, in the case of a single proprietorship). There is no need to go through the BOI, unless incentives are sought. Theoretically, a complete and correct application for registration must be acted upon by the SEC or BTRCP within 15 days of receipt. The SEC's "express lane" acts readily for applicants who are able to use a prepared form. This reduces the filing time for the registration of new corporations to two days if all documentation requirements are submitted with the form. In practice, however, the review generally takes one to three weeks but may be four to six weeks or longer for more complex projects.

The BOI's One-Stop Action Centre (OSAC) facilitates all the inquiries, processing and documentation necessary for foreign investments. It houses under one roof representatives from the government agencies concerned with local and foreign investments, including the BSP, SEC, PEZA and the customs, immigration and labour authorities. Investors are advised to direct their inquiries to the OSAC secretariat. The centre is at the BOI in Metro Manila and is open from 7.00 a.m. to 5.00 p.m. during the weekdays.

Export-oriented projects are the most favoured type of foreign direct investment. They receive the most liberal incentives and may be allowed higher foreign equity ceilings even in areas where such limits are still imposed. Large investment projects in which significant local participation is either required (for example, setting up a finance company or acquiring land) or desirable (for example, local companies that can contribute their expertise in marketing and distribution) may be hindered by a lack of prospective Filipino partners. This is changing as more family-owned corporations shift to professional management under second-generation ownership.

In principle, the Philippines may block foreigners from investing or doing business locally if the other country imposes similar restrictions on Filipinos. This rule, adopted at the height of the Cold War, was intended to apply mainly to nationals of the former communist countries. In practice, it has never been applied.

A foreign investor must obtain BOI approval to take advantage of government investment incentives. To get additional incentives for locating in an export zone or industrial estate, an investor must register with the PEZA. Investors with projects to be registered with the BOI and PEZA must present the results of a feasibility study, using a BOI-prescribed format. A foreign investor may also take advantage of additional incentives by locating in either the Subic Bay Freeport or the Clark Special Economic Zone.

Expansion projects usually do not need the prior approval of any government agency unless the company is seeking incentives or needs to increase capital stock, which would require notifying the BOI or the SEC respectively. Companies that seek to bring in foreign exchange to finance an expansion project are advised to inform the central bank of the remittance.

Other Required Permits

All investments involving financial institutions require the prior approval of the BSP. Investments in new insurance and reinsurance companies require registration with the Insurance Commission. Investments in oil and gas exploration projects are governed by the Department of Energy. Investments in potentially polluting industries or in projects that exploit natural resources also require clearance from the Department of Environment and Natural Resources (see appendix B for full addresses of departments).

Investments in air, sea and land transport, telecommunications, and postal services must be endorsed by the Department of Transportation and Communication. Tourism-related investments must be approved by the Department of Tourism. Technology-transfer agreements must be registered with the Bureau of Patents, Trademarks and Technology Transfer.

Maintaining Your Operations

Reporting requirements and amendments to the articles of incorporation: Securities and Exchange Commission (SEC)

Reporting requirements and registration of business/expansion for incentives: Board of Investments (BOI)

Regular tax payments: Bureau of Internal Revenue (BIR)

Registration of Customs Bonded Warehouse: Bureau of Customs (BOC)

Opening of Letter of Credit: Authorised Agent Banks (AAB)

Certificate to import duty-free: Board of Investments (BOI)

Authority to load/certificate of origin: Bureau of Customs, Export Coordinating Division (BCECD)

Information sheets for first-time exporters: Central Bank of Philippines (CB)

Payment of wharfage fees/exemption from payment: Philippine Ports Authority (PPA)

For projects that require construction of plants, buildings or other land improvements, investors may first need to secure a clearance for location issued by the Housing and Land Use Regulatory Board. Investors must also secure building and related permits from the Local Government Unit (for example, city hall or municipal government) where the proposed project is to be constructed. Local government units are also mainly responsible for zoning ordinances that vary from place to place. Clearances usually take one to two weeks to issue. Administrators of the various export-processing zones and industrial estates in the Philippines may facilitate the issuance of building and related permits.

Exporting to the Philippines

Entering the Market
Entering the Philippine market is relatively easy in the beginning, given the many agents and distributors willing to do business with newcomers. Culturally, the Philippines is the most Westernised country in Asia. Filipinos have a strong preference for Western and Japanese products. Quality and a certain uniqueness are associated with these products.

When selling to the Philippines, it is important to establish a presence. It is absolutely necessary for the foreign exporter to have a local partner since the business is strongly based on personal relationships that require frequent contacts. Visiting old clients every other year will not be sufficient. Experience shows that there is a "grace period" for a newcomer to get acquainted with the locals. If acceptance is not gained during this time, the community will slowly force the intruder out.

Agents and Distributors
Agents and distributors are widely used since they offer a low-cost start-up alternative. They can negotiate sales transactions, direct the product upon entry into the Philippines and provide

product services for Philippine customers. The principal is tied to an agent or distributor by a contract, which normally includes the following: identification of the parties to the contract, conditions of cancellation, duration of the contract, products covered by the contract, and the area in which the products will be distributed and for which the agent will be responsible.

There is currently no special legislation relating to foreign principals and local firms. The only relevant regulations provide for the contract to be governed by the laws of the country in which it is implemented. Contracts may be terminated for the following reasons: one of the parties revokes the contract, the agent withdraws, death, dissolution or insolvency by the principal, accomplishing the objectives of the principal, or expiration of the period for which the agent was hired.

Import Policies

Import Restrictions   There are generally few restrictions on imports, although bringing certain goods into the country is regulated or forbidden. These include explosives, munitions, printed materials hostile to the government, pornographic materials, narcotics, gambling paraphernalia and precious metals.

Import Duties   Customs duties range from nothing to 50%. Current import duties have been reduced considerably since the late 1980s. By 1995, the government had lowered tariffs to not more than 30% on all but 120 items. The reduction in tariffs is generally in line with the government's stated goal of moving to a uniform tariff rate of 5% by the year 2004.

The Philippines participates in the Common Effective Preferential Tariff (CEPT) programme, which involves a reduction of tariffs on trade in the countries of the Association of Southeast Asian Nations. The Philippines is also a member of the Asia-Pacific Economic Cooperation forum, whose 18 members have agreed to eliminate tariff and non-tariff barriers by 2010 for industrialised economies and by 2020 for less-developed economies.

Documentation All imports must pass through customs upon entering the Philippines. Freight forwarders or customs brokers are customarily hired to deal with documentation procedures. Required documents generally include: declaration of import entry, commercial invoice, certificate of origin, bill of lading, inward cargo manifest, irrevocable domestic letter of credit or bank guarantee, and a Clean Report of Findings (CRF) from SGS Inspection Services, the government's customs inspectors (for shipments with Freight on Board (FOB) value of US$500 and above).

Exchange Controls As of August 1992, the Philippines has lifted all exchange controls on current account transactions. Exporters, who previously had to sell the majority of their foreign exchange proceeds to the central bank, may now retain up to 100% of such proceeds in foreign currency accounts. However, exchange controls still remain in financing and in certain areas of investment.

Banking and Foreign Exchange

Financial Institutions and Capital Sources
Short and medium-term capital are readily available to all Philippines-based foreign companies depending on their credit standing. To ensure the flow of capital into the economy, foreigners are not allowed to borrow from the domestic capital market for equity purposes. Foreign-owned firms, however, usually have no problems meeting their short-term capital needs locally. The liberalisation of exchange controls has made available short-term capital at attractive rates.

Long-term funds are more difficult to access. Although long-term commercial paper is gaining acceptance in secondary markets, there is a slow increase in bond issues with the stock exchange fast becoming an important source of capital. Raising long-term funds through borrowing remains limited. The terms for such funds normally require that borrowers fall into prescribed areas of activity (for example, infrastructure development projects) as these programmes are mostly funded through loans from multilateral financial institutions, such as the World Bank and the Asian Development Bank, or through official credit from donor countries like Japan and the United States. Although the weighted average local lending rate was 14.8% per annum in 1996, the prime local lending rate rose to 23% in October 1997 as a result of the mid-1997 Southeast Asian currency crisis.

Banking System   The largest financial institutions are universal banks or "unibanks", which are authorised to offer full commercial, merchant and investment banking services. Other institutions include regular commercial banks, thrift banks, insurance companies, investment houses, financial leasing companies and rural banks. Most of these institutions are able to handle the requirements of eligible foreign-owned firms.

To foster greater strength in the banking system, the central bank has encouraged mergers and acquisitions among banks and other financial organisations to create larger banking institutions. Local unibanks are mostly made up of several types of financial houses grouped under a major commercial bank. The largest unibank groups are Metrobank, Bank of the Philippine Islands, Far East Bank, PCI Bank and the United Coconut Planters Bank.[3] Branch banking has also been liberalised by replacing the auction system with a simpler approval process. Each branch, however, is required to meet a minimum capitalisation requirement (about PHP20 million). Through branches, corporate clients of leading

A vibrant Makati financial district, thanks to a more liberalised business environment.

unibanks are assured of the availability of diversified services even in the provinces.

In May 1994, Congress finally passed the Bank Liberalisation Law (RA 7721) that allows, within a five-year period, more than a dozen additional foreign banks to offer full commercial banking services through a branch or in-country wholly-owned subsidiary. In 1995, the monetary authorities permitted 10 foreign banks to operate branches or subsidiaries, in addition to four foreign banks already operating in the country prior to the passage of the legislation. The 10 banks were ANZ Banking Group, Bangkok Bank, Bank of Tokyo (which later merged with Mitsubishi Bank), Chemical Bank, Deutsche Bank, Development Bank of Singapore, Fuji Bank, ING Bank (that acquired Barings), International Commercial Bank of China and Korea Exchange Bank. Under the law, subsidiaries of foreign banks can also perform full commercial operations by taking up to 60% equity of a local bank. Three foreign banks—Dao Heng Bank, Banco Santander and China Trust Commercial Bank—have entered the country this way.

The entry of more foreign banks has increased funds in the financial system and helped bring in foreign investment, although domestic banks remain dominant in retail banking services. In addition to the 10 foreign banks, there are 16 offshore banking units and 25 representative offices of foreign financial institutions as of February 1997. Foreign resident banks are not allowed to offer trust services and may not become unibanks.

Short-term Capital Short-term credit facilities are the most active form of financing, of which term loans and short-term promissory notes are popular. These facilities may be sourced from leading unibanks and investment houses, although young foreign companies may initially find the credit investigation a tiresome exercise. Other modes of raising short-term capital include bill-purchase lines or overdrafts, discounting of trade bills, trade acceptances (negotiable time drafts drawn chiefly to finance international trade transactions), sales credits, receivables financing (that is, purchase by a bank of corporate accounts receivable) and intercompany borrowings.

The money market consists of the following: interbank call loans, central bank certificates of indebtedness, treasury bills and bonds, promissory notes issued by banks and quasi-banks, re-purchase agreements, certificates of participation, and commercial paper. Banks and quasi-banks participate in all these activities while institutional and other investors participate in all but the first. Companies wishing to raise funds through the money market are advised to approach legitimate banks and investment houses.

Access to external credit for short-term capital purposes has been liberalised, although the central bank reimposed formal reporting requirements in 1994 on all foreign loans and approval requirements on loans amounting to US$10 million and above. Central bank approval is also required for credits guaranteed by the government for re-lending or repayment using the foreign exchange resources of local banks. Foreign credit guarantees are authorised only for projects and industries in preferred areas.

Medium and Long-term Capital   These funds are administered mostly by government financial institutions, particularly the Development Bank of the Philippines, through on-lending or equity participation, usually to projects that fit in with government development plans. As most of these monies are partly funded by concessional loans from multilateral financial agencies (such as the World Bank and the Asian Development Bank), long-term funds are reserved for funding capital equipment purchases and similar project-related activities undertaken by companies that are at least 60% owned by Filipinos.

Foreign companies rarely gain access to these funds. The BSP Circular 1389 issued in 1992 prohibits foreign companies borrowing from local sources for equity purposes. However, the monetary authorities recently repealed the BSP Circular 572, which imposed limits—through debt-to-equity ratios—on the amount of loans that foreign companies with 5% or more foreign equity could borrow domestically.

Long-term capital resources, however, should become less scarce for foreign companies over the next few years. Aside from scrapping the debt-to-equity ratio required of foreign firms borrowing locally, there has also been a notable increase in the acceptability of long-term (three-year) commercial paper in the secondary market. Companies that announced commercial paper issues for 1997 include Metro Pacific, a local flagship of the First Pacific Group of Hong Kong, and Mariwasa Manufacturing, which makes glazed ceramic tiles. Interest rates on commercial paper vary, depending on the rate of the 91-day treasury bill prevailing during the last auction of the previous quarter.

The government-owned Development Bank of the Philippines is the traditional source of long-term funds for industrial borrowers.

As a favoured conduit of medium and long-term funds generated internally, as well as sourced from external lenders such as the World Bank's International Finance Corporation (IFC) and the Asian Development Bank (ADB), the bank finances high-priority agricultural and industrial projects, supports private development banks, supplies public-works loans to the government, and provides financing for real estate development.

Other government-owned financial institutions that lend medium and long-term funds include the Land Bank of the Philippines, which was created to finance the implementation of the comprehensive agrarian reform programme and (to an extent) the Government Service Insurance System, as well as the Social Security System (SSS).

Most private financial institutions also have medium and long-term borrowing windows, although lately they prefer to invest excess lendable funds in high-yielding government securities and short-term lending. Large private investment houses —BPI Capital, AB Capital and Investment, AEA Development and PCI Capital— also provide medium and long-term financing, often through loan syndication.

Insurance companies are a source of mortgage loan capital for industrial buildings. Private development banks, thrift banks and some rural banks are also important sources of capital.

The entry of more foreign banks has forced local financial institutions to gear up for increased competition; hence more innovative financing techniques and lending programmes can be expected. For instance, financing and leasing companies, although still heavily regulated, may become more active.

Exchange Controls

The exchange rate of the Philippine peso is left to float against a "basket" of currencies. The peso's value against the US dollar makes up most of the basket as almost all of the country's external trade and debt obligations are denominated in dollars. The BSP actively participates in the market even in cases of marginal fluctuations, propping up either the peso or the dollar as it sees fit. The monetary board, which is headed by the BSP governor, determines and implements all exchange policies and controls.

The Philippine Dealing System (PDS) is the country's off-floor foreign exchange trading system and has 48 local and foreign commercial banks as members. The reference exchange rate is determined by the weighted average of all foreign exchange transactions fixed by the PDS at 5.30 p.m. on the previous regular banking day. All major currencies can be traded in the spot and forward markets, although transactions in US dollars may account for as much as 95% of the daily turnover. Other currencies traded are (in order of frequency) the yen, the Deutschmark, the pound sterling, the Hong Kong dollar and the Swiss franc.

The monetary board lifted foreign exchange regulations on current-account transactions in September 1992. Further reforms were effected in April 1993. Foreign currencies may now be bought and sold freely by residents (including foreign corporations operating in the Philippines) and may be brought into or sent out of the country with minimal restrictions. Non-residents may also hold foreign currencies freely. Registered foreign-owned or foreign-controlled corporations need no longer convert their foreign exchange receipts into pesos. Executives of foreign firms may also retain all their remuneration in foreign currency.

On 11 June 1996, the president passed the Republic Act 8183, which repealed the 1950 Uniform Currency Law (RA 529) that required all legal obligations in the Philippines to be paid in gold or in Philippine currency. RA 8183 decreed that other currencies may be used as legal tender in the Philippines by providing relief to industries that cater to export markets as well as flexibility to prospective investors. Several insurance companies started offering dollar-denominated policies following the passage of the law.

Meanwhile, the central bank has relaxed the documentation requirements for residents who purchase foreign currency for non-trade purposes like travel, educational and health needs, maintenance of dependants abroad, gifts, subscriptions, rentals, insurance fees, remittance of non-residents' salaries, advertising costs, emigrants' assets transfer, royalties, and rentals.

On 16 January 1997, BSP Governor Gabriel Singson announced that the Monetary Board had raised the ceiling on the amount of foreign exchange that residents may purchase from banks without previously required documentary proofs (for example, airline tickets, hospital bills and school receipts) from US$25,000 to US$50,000. Under existing rules, purchases of more than US$25,000 up to US$6 million must be registered with the BSP while those exceeding US$6 million need prior BSP approval. The BSP move has helped curb non-bank currency purchases and correct the inequality between those who purchase dollars from banks and those who have international currency accounts and credit cards.

The foreign exchange needs of most businesses can be met by local commercial banks at free-market rates. At least 48 banks operate foreign currency deposit units (FCDUs) under the Expanded Foreign Currency Deposit System (EFCDS); among their other privileges, the banks operating the units are allowed to lend foreign exchange domestically.

In addition, there are at least 16 licensed offshore banking units of major foreign banks (though only 15 were operational as of February 1997), which can grant foreign currency loans to non-bank residents—including resident foreign corporations—to finance import or export Letters of Credit (L/Cs).

Although foreign currency transactions have been liberalised, approval by the central bank is required for inward and outward remittance of Philippine pesos in amounts exceeding PHP10,000 (about US$300). The monetary board reimposed this limit to curb trading in pesos in other Asian markets.

The Philippine Constitution of 1987 and several laws, including the 1987 Omnibus Investments Code, guarantee that dividends, interest, loan principal and capital for foreign investments may be remitted.

Taxation

Corporate Taxes

Businesses are subject to manufacturer or producer's sales and income taxes. Non-resident foreign corporations (that is, corporations that are not engaged in trade or business in the Philippines) are taxed only on their income from Philippine sources. Such corporations are taxed at 35% (flat rate) of gross income with no allowable deductions. Interest income on foreign loans earned by non-resident foreign corporations is subject to a 20% tax.

Resident foreign corporations with operations in the Philippines are taxed in the same way as non-resident corporations. The after-tax profits remitted by a Philippine branch of a resident foreign corporation to its head office abroad are subject to a 15% tax, unless the corporation is registered with the PEZA.

Branches are taxed on income derived only from Philippine sources. Subsidiary remittances to the parent office are taxed at 35%. A branch is required to deposit PHP100,000 to the Securities and Exchange Commission after the issuance of its licence. No such requirement is imposed on a subsidiary.

Companies may also be responsible for the following taxes:

- Capital gains taxes of 5% are imposed on the amount realised from the sale of real property to individuals and 10% on the sale or exchange of shares of stock in any domestic corporation, if the amount of the gain is PHP100,000 or less, and 20% if the amount exceeds PHP100,000.
- Local taxes are levied by different provinces (that is, provincial government taxes of 50% of 1% of the total assessed value).
- Overseas communications taxes of 10% are imposed on the

amount paid for communication transmitted from the Philippines,
such as phone calls and fax transmissions.

• Property taxes are charged on commercial, industrial or mineral
lands at 50% of the fair market value. For agricultural lands, the
tax is 40% and for timber, forest and residential lands, the tax
charged is 20%.

Personal Income Taxes

The Philippine Government taxes its citizens on their worldwide
income. A non-resident individual is taxed only on income derived
from sources within the Philippines. The tax rate on taxable income
up to PHP500,000 is 29% and for income over PHP500,000,
it is 35%.

Other Taxes

There is a value-added tax (VAT) of 10% imposed on sales and
transactions of taxable goods as well as on selected services. The
VAT rate of 10% is also imposed on imported goods whether for
use in businesses or for private consumption. Several businesses
and products are exempt from VAT, including "small enterprises",
companies selling non-food agricultural, marine or forest products
in their original state, as well as books and regular periodicals.

Tax Treaties

The Philippines currently has tax treaties that prevent double
taxation with 20 countries. Generally, these treaties cover national
income taxes but not city or municipality taxes.

Manpower and Labour Relations

In 1996, the Philippine labour force totalled more than 29.7
million, with about 27.4 million classified as employed, yielding a
national unemployment rate of 7.5%, down from 8.8% in 1995.
The rate of under-employment has been estimated at 21.5%. The

Where to Go for Permits, Clearances and Registration

- **Expatriates' visas**: Bureau of Immigration
- **Alien Employment Permit**: Department of Labour and Employment
- **Clearance for garment export/quota**: Garments & Textile Export Board
- **Registration for operation of Customs Bonded Manufacturing Warehouse**: Bureau of Customs
- **Environmental compliance certification**: Environmental Management Bureau, Department of Environment and Natural Resources
- **Projects involving land use/conversion**: Housing & Land Use Regulatory Board, National Housing Authority, Department of Agrarian Reform
- **Permit to construct/operate pollution-control devices**: Department of Environment and Natural Resources
- **Trademarks/patents registration**: Bureau of Patents, Trademarks, & Technology Transfer
- **Registration of power generation projects**: National Power Corporation
- **Philippine Standard quality mark to ensure locally made consumer products conform to Philippine standards**: Bureau of Product Standards
- **Import Commodity Clearance Quality Mark to ensure locally made products conform to Philippine standards**: Bureau of Product Standards
- **Clearance for food and chemical projects**: Bureau of Food and Drug
- **Registration of tourism projects**: Department of Tourism
- **Franchise for mass transit operation**: Land Transportation, Franchising and Regulatory Board
- **Telecommunications project**: National Telecommunications Commission
- **Licence/clearance for defence-related projects**: Department of National Defence/Philippine National Police
- **Registration of advanced technology**: Department of Science and Technology
- **Clearance for health-related projects**: Department of Health
- **Clearance for oil exploration activities**: Office of Energy Affairs
- **Acquiring mining rights**: Bureau of Mines & Geo-Sciences
- **Clearance for animal export**: Bureau of Animal Industry

National Statistics Office projects an annual average of 850,000 entrants to the labour force between now and 2010. Expected foreign direct investment inflows will not be adequate to absorb this growth.

The workforce has a high literacy rate, good grasp of English and exhibits readiness in regard to training. Overseas workers deployed from the Philippines contribute substantially to the local economy through remittances. For example, overseas contract workers remitted about $5.1 billion from January to September 1996, up from $4.9 billion for the whole of 1995, according to the BSP and the National Statistics Office. The competition posed by other cheap-labour countries and the more stringent screening of employment contracts and applicants have recently contributed to a downturn in the number of new overseas worker deployments.

The supply of professional, technical and skilled workers, and managers is generally adequate. Recruitment is generally done through newspaper and other printed advertisements, although news of job openings is still spread by word of mouth or announced in notices posted at factory gates (particularly for labour-intensive firms, such as those in garment manufacturing, food processing and even semiconductor assembly). There are relatively few problems with turnover or absenteeism in multinational corporations and foreign-owned companies, as these firms pay relatively high wages.

Labour Laws

Current labour laws are reasonable and should not pose any unusual problems for investors. With subsequent amendments, the Labour Code of the Philippines (PD 442, effective February 1976) consolidates all labour-related legislation. Recent major amendments to the code were the New Labour Relations Law (RA 6715, effective March 1989), the Act Strengthening Prohibition on Discrimination against Women (RA 6725, effective May 1989) and the Wage Rationalisation Act (RA 6727, effective duly 1989).

RA 6715, in particular, aims to bolster protection for workers, strengthen their rights to organise, strike and conduct collective bargaining, promote voluntary modes of dispute settlement, and reorganise the National Labour Relations Commission (NLRC), which has jurisdiction over cases involving employer-employee relations so as to professionalise its ranks and bring its services closer to disputing parties.

The act provides for a five-year collective bargaining agreement, a tripartite NLR, a strike ban in hospitals, direct election of national union officials, supervisor unions, payment of full back wages and benefits for workers deemed to have been illegally dismissed, power of a labour arbiter to order immediate reinstatement of a dismissed employee, and union membership even for newly hired workers.

The Labour Code recognises various unfair practices (including discrimination against women) and bargaining deadlocks as grounds for strikes and lockouts. Suppression of labour rights is a criminal offence. These policies contribute to a conciliatory stance on the part of employees and employers alike.

Working Hours

The normal working week in the manufacturing sector is 44–48 hours. A 40-hour working week is observed in other sectors and is mandatory in the public sector.[4] Workers must be allowed one day's rest out of every seven consecutive days.

The minimum overtime rate is 25% over the hourly rate. Workers on duty on a rest day or a gazetted holiday must be paid a 50% premium over their regular rate for the first eight hours and a 60% premium after that. Workers are paid their normal daily wage during unworked regular holidays. If they work on a holiday, the pay is 30% over the regular rate.

Night-shift employees are entitled to payment of a differential of not less than 10% of the regular rate for work performed between 10.00 p.m. and 6.00 a.m.

Part-time and Temporary Help

Although the country's Labour Code does not contain any specific provision allowing part-time and temporary help, the government does not prohibit employers from engaging in this practice. Employers normally hire extra personnel on a temporary or casual basis for a renewable three to six-month term.

Another prevalent practice is the so-called "labour-only contracting" or LOC, where employers contract labour from agencies that supply specific types of workers. Labour groups contend that Article 106 of the Labour Code bans the practice but the government argues that the provision is unclear on the subject. Labour representatives recently filed House Bill 5490 banning the practice more categorically but the measure is unlikely to become law at this time. In the meantime, the Department of Labour and Employment (DOLE) has indicated that it will consider allowing LOC on a limited basis.

The Labour Code clearly allows for the hiring of apprentices and trainees. Apprentices may be hired only by employers in highly technical industries for a maximum of six months.

The hiring of apprentices is possible only under the auspices of an apprenticeship programme approved by the DOLE. The salary paid should not be below 75% of the existing minimum wage, although the department can authorise the hiring of apprentices without compensation if the training is required by a school. As an incentive to the sponsoring firm, 50% of the value of training cost can be deducted from the firm's taxable income (subject to an overall limit of 10% of the firm's direct wage costs).

Wages and Fringe Benefits

The Wage Rationalisation Act (RA 6727, effective July 1989) created regional tripartite wage and productivity boards to determine and fix minimum wage rates at the regional, provincial and industry levels. This was intended to attract firms to regions with lower wage rates and in the process, disperse industries to the countryside.

As of May 1997, the minimum daily wage rate was PHP185 (equivalent to US$7) for non-agricultural workers in Metro Manila.[5] Average minimum daily wage rates for non-agricultural workers in other regions ranged from PHP116 to PHP155 in 1996. Minimum daily wage rates for agricultural workers in the Manila region was PHP167 (US$6.33) for plantation workers and PHP158.50 (US$6.01) for non-plantation workers. During 1996, the lowest rates found outside Metro Manila were PHP88.30 (US$3.35) for plantation workers and PHP77.10 (US$2.92) for non-plantation workers. The latest raises were ordered in January 1997 by the wage boards for Metro Manila and Southern Mindanao. The other wage boards were expected to increase the foregoing 1996 rates before May 1997 but any raise was unlikely to exceed the 12% hike ordered by the Metro Manila wage board.

Several establishments are exempt from complying with the orders of the wage boards. Among these are distressed companies, new business enterprises and service establishments employing fewer than 10 people, and firms affected by natural disasters. The new rules stipulate that establishments seeking exemptions must apply to the regional wage boards, which will conduct public hearings on the petitions before making a decision.

There is increasing debate over whether regional wage setting actually disperses employment to the countryside. Most regional manufacturing firms are branches of Manila-based companies and consider local market demand and basic infrastructure to be more important determinants of location than wages. Under RA 8188, which amended the Wage Rationalisation Act, employers ignoring the orders of the wage boards face jail terms of between two and four years, plus a fine of not less than PHP25,000 (about US$730). Liable for criminal charges are the establishment's president, vice-president, chief executive officer, general manager or managing director, or their equivalents. Despite such penalties, many employers do not comply with rates set by the wage boards. However, no one seems to have been punished. Stricter monitoring by the DOLE, however, seems to be improving compliance.

Fringe benefits normally add up to 30% of employers' monthly salary and wage expenses. Standard social security benefits include disability pension, retirement pension, a funeral benefit of PHP6,000 (about US$175), sickness allowance, maternity leave of 45 days and maternity pay of up to PHP6,000, and miscellaneous loans (for advances, education, emergencies and so on) of up to PHP8,000 (about US$230). In addition, the Philippine Medical Care Plan provides hospitalisation and other medical benefits. All private sector and government employees are also entitled to a 13th-month salary provided at the end of each calendar year. In June 1996, Congress passed Republic Act 8187, granting paternity leave of seven days with full pay to all married male employees in the private and public sectors for their wives' first four deliveries.

Private-sector employees may retire at the age set in the collective-bargaining agreement or other employment contracts. Generally, employees can retire after 20 years of service. Retirement at age 65 is compulsory in government service; optional retirement at age 60 is preferred. Guidelines in connection with the Retirement Pay Law (RA 7641) provide that retirement pay for every private-sector employee should be equivalent, at least, to one-half of his monthly pay multiplied by every year of service. Retirees are entitled to a portion of the 13th month's pay that is required by law, plus the equivalent of not more than five days of service-incentive leave. The rules stipulate that employers may substitute the PAG-IBIG Fund for the retirement plan, provided this is not against any collective bargaining agreement.[6] Retail, service and agricultural establishments employing fewer than 10 people are exempt from providing the required retirement benefits.

Termination of Employment
The Labour Code lists five grounds for dismissing an employee. They are:

- Gross and habitual neglect of duties
- Committing a crime against the employer, an immediate member of the employer's family or a representative duly authorised by the employer
- Serious misconduct or wilful disobedience of the employer's lawful orders in connection with the employee's work
- Fraud or wilful breach of trust reposed in the worker by the employer
- Installation of labour-saving devices, redundancy or retrenchment to prevent losses or cessation of operations

Regulations require that the DOLE be given one month's notice of the termination of employee services. A worker dismissed because of the installation of a labour-saving device is entitled to separation pay equivalent to at least one month's pay for every year of service.

In cases of retrenchment to prevent losses or closure, or the cessation of operations not caused by serious business losses or financial reverses, the worker must receive separation pay equal to half a month's pay for every year of service or one month's pay, whichever is higher.

All new workers face a probationary period, generally not exceeding six months. The employer may then decide to retain or dismiss the employee. Management may not replace workers who go on strike, even if they defy orders to return to work issued by the DOLE.

The general principle of "no work, no pay" applies to workers displaced from their jobs as a result of calamities such as earthquakes and volcanic eruptions. However, Filipinos traditionally look to their employers for help during such times of calamities.

If a workplace is determined to be unsafe, workers have the right to refuse to report to work. In turn, although employers have no right to compel workers to work, workers will not be entitled to compensation.

Industrial Relations

Most trade unions are in the manufacturing sector. There are three major labour federations: the Federation of Free Workers, the Trade Union Congress of the Philippines and the left-leaning "Kilusang Mayo Uno" (May 1st Movement).

As of October 1996, there are 7,597 active unions in the private sector (total membership exceeds 3.4 million). Around 413,000 workers are covered by 3,445 existing collective bargaining agreements.

The labour situation has remained manageable because of clear-cut government policies, effective enforcement of labour laws and improved management-labour relations as companies get used to collective bargaining. Internal conflicts within and among labour federations and unions also tend to temper local trade unionism. Strikes are usually prompted by unfair labour practices or bargaining deadlocks.

Unfair practices most often cited include harassment of union members, union busting, violations of labour standards and collective agreements, particularly on wages, overtime pay and allowances, and recognition of trade unions. Such violations have been more frequent among Philippine companies than among multinational corporations.

The frequency of walk-outs has been decreasing. The National Conciliation and Mediation Board (NCMB) reported 88 actual strikes in 1996 compared with 97 in 1995 and 99 in 1994. The number of worker-days lost to actual strikes fell from 11% to 520,000 in 1996 as compared to 584,000 in 1995 (as fewer workers were involved in strikes in 1996). Up to 881 unions filed strike notices in 1996, down from 995 the year before.

Government figures also show that government-assisted arbitration is often more effective than internal arbitration between management and employees. The NCMB was reported to have settled 662 of the 786 cases in which it undertook preventive mediation as of October 1996. But only 216 or 53.2% of the 406 cases left to voluntary arbitration were resolved.

Immigration and Customs

Immigration Regulations

Although national policy favours local skills and manpower resources, the state permits foreign participation in employment. This is in line with its policy to attract foreign investment. The government has liberalised visa requirements for certain categories of aliens, including foreign shareholders, investors, representatives of investment houses, land developers and tourism developers. Foreign technicians may be admitted into the country with a prearranged employment visa if the skills they possess are not available in the Philippines.

A foreigner entitled to enter the country under the provisions of a treaty of amity, commerce and navigation may be admitted as a non-immigrant with a treaty-trader visa. This visa enables the foreigner to either carry on substantial trade principally between the Philippines and the state of which he/she is a national, or to develop and direct the operations of an enterprise in which the foreigner is investing or has invested a large amount of capital.

A special investor's resident visa may be issued to any alien with proven Philippine investments of at least US$75,000 (which may be lowered to US$50,000 if the investment is for tourism). Holders of such visas may reside in the Philippines for as long as the investment is maintained. The BOI's One-Stop Action Centre processes special non-immigrant and prearranged employment visas, as well as alien employment permits and the special investor's resident visa.

Firms registered with the BOI and the PEZA may employ foreign nationals in supervisory, technical and advisory positions for five years. This may be extended for limited periods. Foreign personnel of regional or area headquarters and firms locating in export-processing zones, including their spouses and unmarried children under 21 years of age, are issued multiple-entry visas as non-immigrants. They are exempt from immigration fees, alien-registration laws, alien certificates of registration and all other types of clearances, except a tax clearance. The latter can be secured from the Bureau of Internal Revenue upon final departure.

Executive Order 48 permits foreigners (except those of certain restricted nationalities) to stay in the Philippines for up to 21 days without a visa. With a temporary visitor's visa, foreigners may stay in the Philippines for a period of 59 days. This can be extended to a year. Those extending their stay beyond 59 days must register with the Bureau of Immigration and Deportation or, in areas outside Metro Manila, with the office of the local municipal or city treasurer. A foreigner admitted as a non-immigrant can apply for permanent status without having to leave the Philippines.

Customs Regulations

Pre-shipment Inspection   The Bureau of Customs requires a pre-shipment inspection report ("clean report of findings") issued by SGS Inspection Services, the government's contracted customs inspectors, for all imports valued at over US$500. This pre-shipment inspection will be undertaken by the local SGS Inspection Services office prior to shipment from the country of the exporter. SGS inspection includes:

- Physical inspection of goods in the country of supply, including the verification of the quality, quantity and type of goods against the shipping documents

- Reporting the dutiable value of the goods as defined by the Tariff and Customs Code of the Philippines
- Reporting the SGS opinion of the tariff classification of the goods
- Issuing a Clean Report of Findings (CRF) for the purpose of customs clearance

SGS makes a recommendation to the Philippine customs concerning the value and tariff classification. The procedure aids local customs and decreases corruption, thereby also protecting the interests of the trading partners.

In 1996, the Philippine Government abolished the use of the previous customs valuation practice based on "Home Consumption Value", adopted the interim use of "export value" and authorised a shift to the use of "transaction value" before the year 2000.

As a general rule, all goods valued over $500 FOB have to be checked. There are exemptions for used or second-grade goods, or goods that will be temporarily taken to the Philippines for trade exhibitions or for maintenance use, but it is still necessary to have proof of their value from the customs of origin.

The government takes care of all the direct expenses caused by the inspection. Pre-shipment inspection has to be taken into consideration when making service contracts with Philippine companies. Goods arriving into the country without the inspection are subject to seizure.

The role of the exporter is to contact the local SGS office to schedule the pre-shipment inspection. Some time has to be reserved for this, but there are also "express lanes" for emergency situations. The Letter of Credit is a good method of payment as opening it automatically triggers the SGS in the exporting country.

For some exporters, SGS inspection represents additional bureaucracy and costs. For others, it merely represents increased security with the trading transactions. The Philippine Government has a contract with SGS until 1998 and there is some speculation that it would not be renewed. For example, Indonesia recently stopped requiring SGS inspection for its imports.

A local partner can be very helpful when dealing with customs. The recommendations given by SGS are not binding and it is possible that further difficulties may arise.

Import Duties

A key aspect of the government's economic reform programme is to liberalise the import control system by gradually opening up the economy to foreign competition. The programme calls for a shift away from quantitative restrictions towards a primarily tariff-based import control regime. Further liberalisation of import regulations can be anticipated when the authorities bring trade policy in line with the WTO agreement. Around 90% of all product categories are freely importable items that do not require prior approval from the central bank.

Currently, the tariff structure is four-tiered: finished goods produced locally are subject to a 30% tariff rate, those not produced locally, 20%, intermediate goods, 10% and raw materials, 3%. However, some 200 strategic products, including tobacco, rice, coconuts, sugar, fresh fruit and certain luxury consumer goods, remain subject to a 50% tariff rate.

A value added tax (10%) is further included in the price. Generally, lower tariffs are available for goods covered under multilateral agreements, such as the WTO, APEC and especially the ASEAN Free Trade Area (AFTA). The AFTA agreement will significantly lower tariffs in the future, targeting an average of 2.6% by 2003.

Environmental Regulations

The country's environmental rules are contained in the Philippine Environmental Policy (PD 1151) and the Philippine Environmental Code (PD 1152). They establish a system of environmental-impact statements and address other environmental management issues (PD 1586). Pollution control has been a national concern since 1964.

Based on these laws, environmentally critical projects (projects that can cause damage to the environment) must secure an Environmental Compliance Certificate from the Environmental Management Bureau, which is a division of the Department of Environment and Natural Resources (DENR). Environmental-impact statements are mandatory for ventures involving petroleum and petrochemicals, metals and smelting, mining, quarrying and other forms of resource extraction, forest products, fisheries, infrastructure, and projects located at or near environmentally critical areas such as national parks, watershed reserves, wildlife preserves and the ancestral homes of the country's cultural minorities. Other critical industries include textiles, pulp and paper, food processing, and machinery manufacturing and assembly.

Increased public attention on environmental issues reflects the critical levels of pollution in some areas. However, Philippine environmental laws remain fairly limited and enforcement is often lax, particularly after the stage of securing original clearances.

The BOI has set up an environmental support unit (ESU) to assist investors in obtaining environmental-compliance certificates (ECCs). The ESU includes a representative of the DENR, who serves as both a liaison officer and consultant to facilitate the process.

The move comes in the wake of a growing number of BOI-registered companies—most notably cement manufacturers and tourist-resort developers—securing ECCs from the Environmental Management Bureau.

In December 1996, President Ramos approved the revisions to the Implementing Rules and Regulations (IRR) of the 1995 Philippine Mining Act. The DENR was forced to revise the IRR after a huge spill of toxic mine tailings from the facilities of Marcopper Mining (owned partly by Canada's Placer Dome) engulfed the Boac River in Marinduque province in March 1996. The accident destroyed the livelihood and threatened the health of up to 700 families.

The IRR gives local governments the right to approve small-scale mining and quarrying in their areas and participate in the decision-making and monitoring of mining operations. It rejects mining applications for built-up areas or for portions of land within municipalities or for districts actually occupied as residential, commercial or industrial areas.

The rules require a minimum capitalisation of $4 million on foreign mining companies applying for a Financial and Technical Assistance Agreement, which is a contract with the government involving financial or technical assistance for large-scale exploration, development and utilisation of mineral resources.

As of January 1997, other new items in the revised IRR require mining companies to take the following steps:

- Submit a detailed comprehensive and strategic environmental management plan, including protection and rehabilitation of the disturbed environment during the exploration period
- Post an environmental guarantee fund to compensate for damages in case of violations of environmental laws
- Allocate at least 10% of total project costs for environmental related capital expenditure
- Seek the "informed consent" of indigenous people and other communities to be affected by the mining operation before entering their lands, and pay them a minimum royalty fee of 1% of gross output
- Allocate 1% of their annual mining/milling costs for community development projects

Protection of Investments and Intellectual Property

Since President Ramos took over the reins of government, the Philippine economy has opened itself to foreign investors in order to strengthen its competitiveness. Many government-operated companies, monopolies and other arrangements that have restricted competition have been removed while the capital market has been liberalised. This privatisation programme has achieved success and foreign investments have multiplied recently.

At the international level, the Philippines has signed the convention, which establishes the Multilateral Investment Guarantee Agency (MIGA), the Settlement of Investment Disputes between States and Nationals of Other States, and the New York Convention on Recognition of Foreign Arbitral Awards. In cooperation with the ASEAN member-countries, several conventions in regard to investments have also been signed.

The protection of intellectual rights in the Philippines is probably more effective than in most countries in Southeast Asia. In April 1993, a major step forward was taken when the Philippines and the United States signed an agreement to strengthen the protection of intellectual property rights in the Philippines. The Philippines was moved from the Special 301 "priority watch list" to the "watch list". It is a member of the Paris Convention for the Protection of Industrial Property and the World Intellectual Property Organisation.

Both patents and trademarks must be registered with the Bureau of Patents, Trademarks and Technology Transfer. Patents may be granted for five to 17 years. Trademarks are valid for 20 years from the registration date and are renewable for similar periods. The owner must file an affidavit every five years asserting that the trademark is being used. The examination procedure includes a 30-day opposition period after filing the application.

The Philippine Code of Commerce includes provisions on merchandise, commerce, maritime commerce, certain types of commercial contracts, insolvency law, commercial registries and bookkeeping. The Philippine Code of Corporations includes provisions on incorporation and organisation of corporations, board of directors, trustees and officers, power of corporations,

Thinking of Setting-up Shop in Luzon? Consider these distances from Manila

Destination	Kilometres
Bando, Bulacan	16
Cavite City, Cavite	34
Malolos, Bulacan	44
Calamba, Laguna	54
Canlubang, Laguna	55
Tagaytay City, Cavite	56
Los Banos, Laguna	62
Alaminos, Laguna	78
Angeles City, Pampanga	83
Pansanjan, Laguna	101
Paete, Laguna	102
Batangas City, Batangas	111
Balanga, Bataan	123
Sariaya, Quezon	124
Calatagan, Batangas	125
Olongapo City, Zambales	126
Lucena City, Quezon	136
Camiling, Tarlac	159
Alaminos, Pangasinan	182
San Fabian, Pangasinan	230
Baguio City, Mountain Province	246
Bauang, La Union	259
San Fernando, La Union	264
Bagabag, Nueva Vizcaya	287
Santiago, Isabela	329
Banaue, Ifugao	348
Daet, Camarines Norte	350
Narvacan, Ilocos Sur	375
Bontoc, Mountain Province	394
Naga City, Camarines Sur	449
Paoay, Ilocos Norte	470
Batac, Ilocos Norte	471
Iriga City, Camarines Sur	487
Laoag City, Ilocos Norte	487

meetings of the corporation, stocks and stockholders, corporate books and records, merger and consolidation, dissolution, and foreign corporations.

Acquisition of Land

Under the Philippine Constitution, foreigners may not own land. Only Philippine citizens, and corporations and associations in which Philippine citizens own at least 60% of capital may acquire private land. Under the Condominium Law (RA 4726, effective June 1966), foreigners may own no more than 40% of the units in any condominium project.

House Bill 6301 and Senate Bill 1600 proposed the amendment of the 1966 law to allow 100% foreign ownership in condominiums and other property in industrial estates. The property may be factories, buildings, plants, houses or recreational facilities. However, as of early 1997, these bills were still pending in Congress. Points of conflict with the constitution remained unresolved and the proposals have been eclipsed by the congressional passage of a law extending land leases. The Investors' Lease Act (RA 7652, effective June 1993) doubled the maximum initial leasehold period from 25 to 50 years while retaining the possibility of a 25-year renewal. The law applies only to long-term investors for the establishment of industrial estates, factories, assembly or processing plants, agro-industrial enterprises, land development for industrial and commercial use, tourism and other similar projects.

To receive the long-term lease, investments in tourism projects must involve a minimum of US$5 million, 70% of which must be invested within three years from the signing of the lease contract. Prime agricultural lands are not eligible for extended lease.

The Comprehensive Agrarian Reform Law (RA 6657, effective June 1988) required redistribution of land held by foreigners. Lease contracts for lands exceeding 1,000 hectares (for corporations) or 500 hectares (for individuals) were to be amended to conform to constitutional limits. Excess lands were to be redistributed. Smaller parcels under lease to foreign corporations or individuals were subject to redistribution as of 29 August 1992.

CHAPTER 5

Present and Future Niches

In what type of business venture should you involve yourself? According to business people, government officials, investment houses and chambers of commerce, there are four major investment niches to explore when prospecting for super deals in the Philippines. These are:

- The Subic Bay Freeport and the Clark Special Economic Zone
- Public-private partnerships in infrastructure and utilities
- Regional public and private investment hubs for agro-industrial and manufacturing projects
- Tourism estates, accommodation and transportation

Tax, training, residency and foreign employment incentives apply to all four areas under the Republic Act 7916 or the Special Economic Zone Act of 1995.

The "Tantalising" Incentives

- A special tax rate of 5% of gross income in lieu of all national and local taxes
- Additional deduction for training expenses
- Permanent resident status for foreign investors and immediate family
- Employment of foreign nationals

The Ninoy Aquino International Airport in Manila links the country to business from the outside world.

Aside from location, infrastructural and manpower advantages, each of these investment niches offers unique "treats and goodies" that will surely entice any investor. Moreover, what you find missing in one niche might just be offered as a special ingredient in another.

Subic Bay Freeport and Clark Special Economic Zone

As growth among Asia-Pacific countries cools down, alternative hot places to look out for in the region are the transformed Subic Bay Naval Base and Clark Air Base. These former US military installations in the Philippines are now called the Subic Bay Freeport (SBF) and the Clark Special Economic Zone (CSEZ).

In the last four years since the US Armed Forces' departure after the expiration of the 1947 Military Bases Agreement (MBA), these places have gradually metamorphosed to become bases of Philippine economic stability and solid growth—a new mission in a new era of international relations. These past staging areas of US defence operations in the Pacific have now been hailed by corporate leaders of the Philippines as critical growth centres that will push the country's economy forward through much-needed trade and investments.

Since the start of the SBF and the CSEZ's conversion in the early 1990s, international investment consultants and trade analysts, especially those from around the Asia-Pacific region, have predicted a sustained growth of business opportunities for these former military bases. This was definitely good news for Philippine economic planners, who for many years, have been trying unsuccessfully to stir up domestic market activity. Economic data shows that the economy is gaining from these zones, which are integral parts of the Subic-Clark-Manila Buffer Growth Triangle. Many business ventures are attracted to the SBF and the CSEZ because of their inherent advantages: excellent location, committed managers, juicy perks, an abundant human resource pool and world-class infrastructure.

Excellent Location

Strategically located in one of the most economically active regions in the world, Subic Bay Freeport in Olongapo City, Zambales and Clark Special Economic Zone in Angeles City, Pampanga are accessible from major cities in East Asia as the table below illustrates:

Travel Time from Major Cities to the Philippines

Asian City	By Air (hours)	By Ship (days)
Hong Kong	2.00	3
Taipei	2.00	3
Ho Chi Minh	2.30	3
Bangkok	3.00	3
Shanghai	3.25	4
Singapore	3.30	4
Brunei	3.50	4
Tokyo	3.50	4
Jakarta	3.50	4
Seoul	3.50	5
Kuala Lumpur	4.00	7

The Subic Bay Freeport is located approximately 80 km north of Metro Manila. The natural deep harbour is bordered by the Zambales Mountain Range in the east and Subic Bay in the west, opening up to the vast South China Sea. The SBF is north-west of the Bataan Peninsula and south-west of the Zambales Province. Subic Bay covers 14,614 hectares of land. Clark Special Economic Zone is also situated about 80 km north of Manila and is 70 km north-east of the SBF. It occupies prime land in the Pampanga and Tarlac provinces, covering 23,601 hectares.

Committed Managers

Both CSEZ and SBF operate under the umbrella of the Philippines' Bases Conversion Development Authority (BaseCon). At the actual sites, day-to-day operations of SBF are supervised by the Subic Bay Management Authority (SBMA) while Clark Special Economic Zone is handled by the Clark Development Corporation (CDC).

Registration Process for Foreign Enterprise at the Subic Bay Freeport (SBF) and the Clark Special Economic Zone (CSEZ)

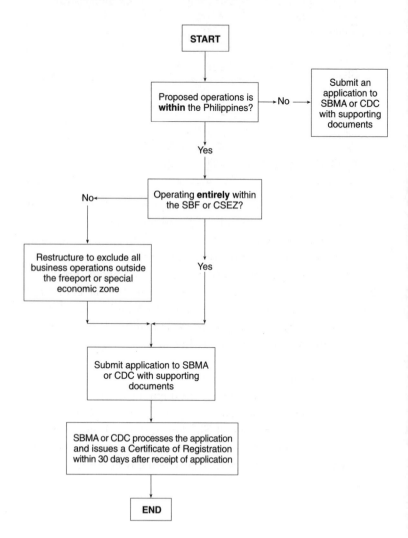

The administration and operations of these zones have solid backing from the national government and local leaders. In terms of leadership, the SBF and CSEZ are led by visionary, committed and action-oriented teams of managers with proven track-records in both the public and the private sectors. The national government, SBMA and CDC administrators, and the private sector are united in the belief that these former US military bases are the super locomotives that will pull the Philippines towards NIC status by the year 2000.

Juicy Perks

Both the CSEZ and the SBF boast liberal trade and investment packages that have enticed global entrepreneurs, especially those who seek to maximise East Asia's consumer booms, emerging markets and regional links. The lucrative investment possibilities seem endless, ranging from manufacturing to tourism and even agriculture. Just like any special economic or freeport zone in the world, these two areas offer attractive investment perks. These include tax-free and duty-free importation of capital equipment, raw materials and finished goods. CSEZ and SBF also offer a liberal banking and foreign exchange regime. Business entry and exit policies have been made relatively simple. In most cases, SBMA and CDC administrators process a business application and issue a Certificate of Registration within 30 days after submission.

A Big Human Resource Pool

A highly-skilled, English-speaking labour pool is readily available. Many are former base workers familiar with both Asian and Western-style management practices. Skilled manpower is abundant in shipbuilding and repair services, electrical works, metalworking, marine and machinery repair, and power plant maintenance.

Established World-class Infrastructure

Aside from incentives and perks, many potential investors are impressed by the world-class infrastructure the two zones inherited from the US Armed Forces. Defence planners and their corps of engineers have created a world-class ancillary infrastructure. For instance, these bases have extensive road networks, power generation and water filtration capabilities, hotels, private villas, housing and office facilities, recreational, shipping and port facilities, international airports, warehouses, fire stations, petroleum storage, and modern telecommunications. In the case of the SBF, the facilities left by the US military would have cost the Philippine Government an estimated US$8 billion to build. A perimeter fence built by the previous occupants provides added security to both zones.

The fast-paced development during the past years has created many beneficial "returns" for entrepreneurs and the host country.

Business!

Interestingly, many American companies are leading the investment charge into the former bases. Federal Express, which made the SBF its Asian hub, now flies delivery sorties in strategic areas previously covered by US tactical fighters. Enron Power Corporation and Coastal Petroleum, two US business giants, run the SBF's power and depot facilities while telecommunications is managed by a joint venture between the Philippine Long Distance Telephone Company (PLDT) and AT&T. However, Americans are not the only ones who have come to these trading havens. Asian and European investors like Universal Lighting (a Russian and US joint venture), Keller Insurance (UK), Acer Computers (Taiwan), Metroplex (Malaysia), Wartsila Diesel (Singapore), Thompson Audio (France), Royal Cargo (Germany), Vision Fashion (Australia) and Nisshin Corporation (Japan) have joined in the trade and investment attack. In both the SBF and the CSEZ, strong support has also been lent by more than 100 Filipino-owned companies.

Revenue!

Subic Bay Management Authority officials expect more than US$1 billion worth of projects from some 204 local and foreign companies. All types of business partnerships are being worked out between public and private, as well as among local and foreign individuals and groups.

To boost the SBF's capacity to achieve its strategic objectives, the World Bank provided a US$40 million loan package to help convert many of the military facilities for commercial use. Meanwhile in Angeles City, the Clark Development Corporation (CDC) has approved proposals from 142 foreign and local companies—63 industrial projects, 49 commercial undertakings, 12 in the service industry, eight in aviation, four in housing, three in utility and three in tourism. As of May 1996, signed lease agreements with the CDC have reached 110 projects valued at close to US$200 million. In retrospect, US military rental payments could not have equalled these current and anticipated revenues.

Jobs!

As a result of these initial surges in investments, a significant number of lost jobs have already been recovered as part of the bases' transformation. According to officials in these two special economic zones, approximately half the jobs lost have already been replaced by the new companies. With careful selection and intensive training, most former Subic Bay and Clark field base personnel have adjusted to the changing needs of their new employers. By the year 2003, the World Bank estimates that more than 80,000 new jobs will be generated—more jobs than what the US military was able to create. Moreover, in the case of Subic

Bay, many of the former base workers continue to volunteer their time to ensure that the freeport and special economic zone become a resounding success.

Public-Private Partnerships in Infrastructure and Utilities

Philippine leaders concur with advisers from the World Bank and Asian Development Bank that for the country to sustain its current economic trajectory, public and private sectors need to increase investments in the infrastructure sector over the next few decades. Hence, this is another niche for business people to explore. With available national and local government partnerships and perks, there continues to be a strong magnetic pull towards infrastructure, and utilities construction and development, especially in the telecommunications, energy, transportation and information technology sub-sectors.

Projected Infrastructure Spending

Sub-sector	Total cost (US$ m)	Period
Telecommunications	27,975	1991–2010
Power	25,370	1995–2000
Roads	1,626	1993–2000
Air transport	806	1995–2001
Water transport	542	1994–1999
Water/sewer facilities	463	1993–2000

Projects and programmes in these areas can be started up using straightforward public-private partnership schemes known as BOTs (Build-Operate-and-Transfers). There are nine basic types of BOT schemes, with joint venture and other partnership arrangements that have also been given the go-ahead by the government.

Build-Operate-and-Transfer (BOT)

This is the most common contractual arrangement between the government and a potential investor. The project proponent carries out the financing, construction, operation and maintenance of an infrastructure facility. The project proponent operates the facility over a fixed term, during which it is allowed to charge facility users appropriate tolls, fees, rentals and charges not exceeding those specified in its contract. Such fees and charges should enable the proponent to recover its investment and to cover operating and maintenance expenses incurred by the project. The facility is transferred to the government agency or local government unit at the end of the fixed term, which shall not exceed 50 years.

More investments are needed to improve the infrastructure sector. Many perks and incentives have been put in place to draw potential investors.

Build-and-Transfer (BT)

A close variant of the BOT arrangement is the BT scheme, wherein the project proponent undertakes the financing and construction of an infrastructure or development facility. But unlike the BOT, after the project is completed, the proponent turns it over to the implementing national government agency or local government unit. This is upon payment to the proponent-developer, using an agreed schedule, of its total investment expended on the project plus a reasonable rate of return.

Build-Lease-and-Transfer (BLT)

In this project arrangement, the proponent is authorised to finance and construct an infrastructure or development facility. Upon project completion, the proponent turns the facility over to the national government agency or local government unit concerned on a lease arrangement for a fixed period. Ownership of the facility is automatically transferred to the national government agency or local government unit after the specified period.

Build-Own-and-Operate (BOO)

A BOO partnership is where a private entrepreneur is authorised to finance, construct, own, operate and maintain an infrastructure or development facility, and in return collects tolls, fees or other charges from facility users. The project proponent, which owns the assets of a facility, may assign its operation and maintenance to an operator or contractor.

Build-Transfer-and-Operate (BTO)

In a BTO arrangement, the national government agency or local government unit contracts out the building of an infrastructure facility to a private entity on a turnkey basis. Once the facility is commissioned satisfactorily, the title is transferred to the implementing public agency. Under an agreement, the private entity is authorised to operate the facility on behalf of the national or local government agency.

Contract-Add-and-Operate (CAO)
Another contractual agreement is the CAO, where a project proponent adds on to an existing infrastructure facility by renting it from the national or local government. The investor operates the expanded project over an agreed franchise period. There may or may not be a transfer arrangement on the added facility provided by the proponent.

Develop-Operate-and-Transfer (DOT)
In this scheme, the right to develop an adjoining property is given to the proponent of a new infrastructure project. This lets the proponent enjoy the benefits from the project, such as higher property or rent values.

Rehabilitate-Operate-and-Transfer (ROT)
A ROT partnership requires the private company to refurbish, operate and maintain an existing facility over a franchise period. When this ends, the facility is turned over to the national or local government agency.

Rehabilitate-Own-and-Operate (ROO)
In a ROO arrangement, an existing facility is turned over to the private sector to refurbish and operate with no time imposed on ownership. As long as the operator does not violate its franchise, it can continue operating the facility.

Many public and private partnership projects, mostly in the power sector, have been completed using various BOT schemes and more opportunities are opening up for bids and proposals.

Regional Public and Private Investment Centres for Agro-industrial and Manufacturing

Tired of congested and polluted Metropolitan Manila? Over the years, a number of domestic foreign firms have already made lucrative profits outside Manila through regional public and private investment centres, estates and parks that offer great incentive packages and unique strategic advantages. Aside from the usual national tax, tariff and licensing benefits that other investment niches offer, these centres add more local tax perks and permit perks in addition to relatively low rental and utility rates. These convenient and hassle-free industrial parks and estates are in almost every region of the Philippines. Inside each geographic region are numerous local government units that are now empowered to attract and sustain business and investments.

Ilocos or Region I
This comprises the provinces of Pangasinan, La Union, Ilocos Sur and Ilocos Norte. The Ilocos region is blessed with rich land bordered by the sea on the one side and sheltered by mountains on the other. Occupying the north western area of Luzon, the provinces in the region have some of the most developed infrastructure and support facilities in the country.

The strategically located Bacnotan Regional Industrial Centre in La Union will be the focal point of the region's investment charge. It is located approximately 18 km from San Fernando Airport and Seaport.

Raw materials found in the region are livestock and poultry, fisheries and aquatic resources, rice, tobacco, sugar cane, vegetables, iron (magnetic sand), coal, clay, limestone, sand and gravel. The Bacnotan Regional Industrial Centre has well-established power, water and telecommunications infrastructure. The centre also has amenities like hotel and conference facilities.

Suitable Investment Ventures for Region I

Food processing, ceramics, gifts and household products, yacht and boat manufacturing, agricultural tools and equipment production, and textile mills

Northern Luzon or Region II

This region consists of the provinces of Batanes, Cagayan, Nueva Vizcaya and Quirino. Isabela in Cagayan Province is the designated location of the Cauayan Regional Industrial Centre. Region II is a frontier area noted for its virgin forests, hardy and industrious people, and colourful ethnic minorities. The centre site is an 80-hectare area in Barangay Tagaran. The government has planned both off-site and on-site infrastructure facilities development for the multi-million-dollar centre. It is located 5.3 km from the Cauayan Airport and is 55 minutes flying time from Manila.

There are five other airports in Region II. The nearest seaport is in Santa Ana, Cagayan, with three other alternative ports in the neighbouring provinces. Power, water and telecommunications facilities have recently been installed. Hotel and lodging houses are found in the provinces of Cagayan, Isabela and Nueva Viscaya.

Suitable Investment Ventures for Region II

Wood processing, food processing, agricultural machinery production, garments manufacturing and subcontracting, essential oil processing, machinery/equipment and parts, electrical products, electronic products, metal products and support services, textile and textile products, and leather tanning and leather products, and miscellaneous manufacturing

Central Luzon (or Region III)

This comprises the dynamic provinces of Bataan, Bulacan, Nueva Ecija, Pampanga, Tarlac and Zambales. Growth and investment for the region is expected from the Bataan Export Processing Zone Authority (BEPZ) situated in Mariveles, which is on the southern tip of the Bataan Peninsula facing Manila Bay. Although BEPZ is 160 km from Metropolitan Manila, the available land, air and sea transport services keep it within easy reach. Two bus lines make daily trips to Mariveles; travel time is three hours via a concrete and asphalt road network. From the Manila Domestic Airport, the BEPZ is only 25 minutes away by helicopter. All the other provinces that are within the zone's sphere of operations have a growing population of private industrial estates.

The BEPZ has 11 standard factory buildings that can be leased to light, labour-intensive industries. These buildings have three-storeys, with each floor measuring approximately 3,000 square metres. Each building is equipped with garbage chutes, water tanks and lavatories. Provisions for cargo elevators, electricity and lighting, telephone facilities, and fire alarm systems are in place. Housing, sports and recreational facilities are also available.

There are already a number of established manufacturing industries operating in the BEPZ, manufacturing goods like semi-conductor and electronic products, garments, gifts, toys, footwear, industrial products, seacraft and yacht products, and paper and packaging products mostly for the international markets.

Suitable Investment Ventures for Region III

Food and beverages, wood and wood products, tobacco, fabricated metals, textiles, rubber and plastic products, garments, and miscellaneous manufacturing industries

Southern Tagalog or Region IV

This region is the largest among the country's 14 regional subdivisions. It covers an area of 46,924 sq km or 16% of the country's total area. The region comprises 11 provinces, which include Aurora, Quezon, Laguna, Cavite, Batangas and Rizal in the mainland and the island provinces of Marinduque, Romblon, Palawan, Oriental Mindoro and Occidental Mindoro.

Strategically placed in Batangas City, the Batangas Regional Agro-Industrial Centre (BRAIC) is the beacon for the government's industrial development strategy for this huge and bustling region. The centre is just 5 km away from the Port of Batangas and about 10 km from the Ninoy Aquino International Airport. Power is provided by the Manila Electric Company (MERALCO) while telecommunications support can be secured from Philippine Long Distance Telephone Company (PLDT), Philippine Telephone (PILTEL) and Globetelecom.

Linked to the Southern Tagalog Region's ambitious development plan are other privately developed industrial centres, which include First Cavite Industrial Estate, Light Industry and Science Park of the Philippines (Laguna), Laguna Technopark Inc., Gateway Business Park (Cavite), Luisita Industrial Estate (Tarlac), Carmelray Development Corporation (Laguna), Leyte Industrial Development Estate, and Tabangao Special Export Processing Zone (Batangas). Similarly, these privately developed industrial parks offer a range of locational advantages and tantalising perks that match those offered by the BRAIC and other public parks.

Suitable Investment Ventures for Region IV

Food processing (fish and metal canning, fruit juices, vegetable oil, vegetable-based protein and coffee), garments and sporting goods, chemical products (industrial and agricultural), pharmaceutical, soap and other related products, and metal-based industries (shipbuilding and repair, automotive parts and component, motorcycles, and furniture)

Bicol or Region V

This region is located at the midsection of the country, comprising six provinces, four in the southernmost part of Luzon (Camarines Norte, Camarines Sur, Albay and Sorsogon) and two island provinces (Catanduanes and Masbate). Region V has three major cities: Naga and Iriga in Camarines Sur and Legaspi City in Albay. There are open seas on almost all sides of the Bicol region. Mountains and volcanoes are all part of the resource-rich landscape of the area.

A large segment of the region's agro-industrial strategy will revolve around the Legaspi Industrial Centre in Albay, which will serve as the gateway for trade from the Visayas into Luzon. The centre is only 6 km from the Legaspi National Airport and 10 km from Legaspi's main port. The road network around the site is constantly being upgraded.

Currently, the combined efforts of Local Government Units and various line agencies in the planning and implementation of the Legaspi-Iriga-Naga Growth Corridor aim to link the growth poles of the provinces of Albay and Camarines Sur. Major agro-industrial programmes like the Integrated Crop, Livestock, Dairy and Poultry Development Programme, Integrated Fisheries Development Programme, Integrated Mineral and Agricultural Production Centres, and Integrated Agro and Food-Based Industries Development are already well underway.

Suitable Investment Ventures for Region V

Agri-based industries (sweet potato processing and coconut by-products processing), perlite processing, marble processing, sulphuric acid processing, silica processing, gypsum/plaster of Paris processing, essential oils processing, ice plant and cold storage, industrial salt processing, pulp, paper and paperboard manufacturing, rope, cordage and twine manufacturing, ceramics, and fish and meat processing

Western Visayas or Region VI

This comprises the provinces of Iloilo, Aklan, Antique, Capiz, Negros Occidental and Guimaras. The region's economy is predominantly agricultural. Western Visayas has abundant natural resources, a strategic location and ample room for exploration and expansion. These render the region an attractive proposition to adventurous local and foreign investors.

The region has rich reserves of mineral resources that are still largely untapped commercially. They are iron, gold, silver, chromate, manganese and copper. There are also non-metallic resources like limestone, cement, marble, silica, gypsum, clay sulphur, pyrite, guano, rock phosphate, feldspar and molybdenum.

At the centre of this vast potential region is the Pavia Regional Agro-Industrial Centre, which is just 7.5 km from the airport and 9 km from the nearest seaport at Iloilo City. Existing infrastructure include power, water and telecommunications, as well as social amenities like schools, hospitals, banks and post offices.

The Pavia Regional Agro-Industrial Centre represents the regional growth pole and is core of the Panay-Negros Agro-Industrial Special Development Programme (PANAI-SDP). Resource-based industries moving to Pavia are supported by District Agro-Industrial Centres (DAICs) dispersed strategically all over the region. These DAICs are the main conduits for primary producers and intermediate processors of raw materials.

Suitable Investment Ventures for Region VI

Food and beverage, small-scale wood and furniture businesses, cottage industries, footwear manufacturing, and thresher production

---

Central Visayas or Region VII

This region is made up of four provinces: Cebu, Bohol, Siquijor and Negros Oriental. The first three are independent island provinces while Negros Oriental is separated from Negros Occidental by mountain ranges. The four provinces have irregular coastlines that provide good harbours.

Metro Cebu is the centre of commerce, industry and education in the area. Highly urbanised, it has been dubbed the "Queen City of the South". Its phenomenal growth has caught the attention of development planners and industrialists. Some of the Central Visayas' current economic pursuits include cultivation of commercial crops and development of agro-processing, integrated development of agro-forestry-based products, and integrated development of micro cottage and small enterprises that utilise indigenous raw materials. Economic and education opportunities attract migrants from all over the country.

The main trade hub in the region is the Mactan Export Processing Zone (MEPZ) located 15 km from Cebu City, which is also the nearest seaport. It is just 50 m from Mactan Airport and is just one hour flying time to Manila. Power is supplied to the MEPZ by the National Power Corporation (NAPOCOR) while water is serviced by the Metro Cebu Water District. The MEPZ also has its own deepwells with a capacity of 1,225 litres per minute. Telecommunications for voice, data and facsimile transmissions are in place.

Amenities in the zone include housing facilities, ports, factory buildings, trucking and forwarding services, administrative offices, and sports facilities. For easy registration, the MEPZ functions as a one-stop agency, where representatives from the respective government offices are present to facilitate registration and answer questions regarding other requirements. Moreover, the land lease, industrial power and industrial water rates are some of the most competitive in the country.

Suitable Investment Ventures for Region VII

Aircraft assembly/manufacturing, aircraft rebuilding/ refurbishing, electronic components and semiconductor, food processing, pharmaceutical and other therapeutic preparations, light machinery and precision equipment, plastic production, toy manufacturing, computer assembly, communication equipment/ manufacturing, packaging materials manufacturing, and pleasure seacraft manufacturing

---

Eastern Visayas or Region VIII

This region literally serves as the geographic backbone of the Philippines since it is strategically positioned in the mid-eastern border of the country, connecting the islands of Luzon and Mindanao to the rest of the Visayas through the Maharlika Highway and the world-renowned San Juanico Bridge. It has six provinces: Leyte, Southern Leyte, Bilaran, Samar, Eastern Samar and Northern Samar.

Through the Eastern Visayas Regional Agro-Industrial Growth Centre (EVRGC), local leaders hope that the provinces in the region can jump on the national bandwagon. It offers tremendous pluses to investors like geothermal power, abundant water and raw materials, skilled and trainable manpower, and ready-for-business infrastructure.

The EVRGC is located in bustling Tacloban City and is 20 km from the modern Daniel Z. Romualdez Airport. The nearest seaport is 14 km away. The Eastern Visayas Regional Agro-Industrial Growth Centre is accessible from all parts of the region via a well-maintained road network. Social amenities like restaurants, resorts, hotels, health facilities and housing are conveniently located.

Linked to the Eastern Visayas Regional Agro-Industrial Growth Centre is the Leyte Industrial Development Estate (LIDE).

With 80 hectares of available land, it is already being partially utilised by Alcorn Petroleum, Taiwan Cement and Asia Pacific Gypsum Products Corporation.

Suitable Investment Ventures for Region VIII

Food, beverage, textiles, fabricated metal products, glass, ceramic, non-ferrous metal and electronic/electronic machinery

Western Mindanao or Region IX

This region comprises the island provinces of Basilan, Zamboanga del Norte and Zamboanga del Sur. The key cities in the region are Dapitan, Dipolog and Zamboanga. The region's shoreline stretches for 2,563 km or more than 40% of the entire Mindanao's coastline. It produces 93% of the country's cultured seaweed exports.

The region has the country's largest deposits of lead and zinc, found in the two Zamboanga provinces. Non-metallic minerals like clay, asbestos, limestone, quartz, silica, phosphate, rock, sand and marbles are also found in the region.

The fishing grounds of western Mindanao produce fish varieties such as slipmouths, moonfishes, big-eyed and round scads, round herrings, sardines, anchovies, frigate tuna, ship jocks, mackerels, and hairtails.

The Zamboanga City Regional Agro-Industrial Centre is only 12 km from Zamboanga City International Airport, which is also the hub of domestic travel to the region. The main seaport is just 15 km away. Infrastructure facilities include modern water, power, telecommunications and road systems.

Promising and lucrative business opportunities centre on aquaculture production and processing. The Philippines is a global leader in the production of seaweed and it is only one of the four countries in the world that is capable of producing completely refined seaweed.

In terms of location, the Zamboanga City Regional Agro-Industrial Centre is closer than any other industrial park in the country to Malaysia, Brunei, Singapore and Indonesia, which are important markets for Philippine products.

Aside from the proximity to these ASEAN neighbours, the centre is nearest to one of the busiest sea lanes in the world—the Straits of Malacca. Foreign vessels use the Straits of Malacca to pass to and from the continents of Asia, Europe, Australia and the Americas. This is a big edge for prospective investors who greatly value the Asia-Pacific export market and its global linkages.

Suitable Investment Ventures for Region IX
Seaweed processing, food processing, tobacco processing, garment manufacturing, machine and equipment fabrication, gifts, toys and houseware (shell-based), marine products, electrical products, agricultural tools and equipment, yacht/boat manufacturing, and textile mills

---

Northern Mindanao or Region X

This region is considered one of the most promising regions in the country and has seven provinces: Agusan del Norte, Agusan del Sur, Bukidnon, Camiguin, Misamis Occidental, Misamis Oriental and Surigao del Norte. Northern Mindanao has 1,160 km of coastline and 176,200 hectares of inland water area suitable for fresh and brackish water aquaculture, as well as fish-capture operations. Thirty-four percent of the total land area is devoted to agriculture, making agri-based industries ideal in terms of access to important raw material sources. Metallic and non-metallic minerals also abound in the region. Two ferro-alloy plants and a nickel refinery are already in operation.

An integral component of the Metro Cagayan Special Development Project is the Phividec Industrial Estate-Misamis Oriental (PIE-MO) in Cagayan de Oro, which is run by one of

the country's well-established industrial estates managers—
Phividec (Philippine Veterans Investment Development
Corporation). The PIE-Misamis Oriental is 28 km away from the
Cagayan de Oro Airport and 22 km from the Port of Cagayan de
Oro. Water, power, telecommunications and road infrastructures
are some of the most reliable and competitively priced in the
region. Additional support facilities include flood control and
drainage systems, electrical lines, water and sewage systems, and
solid waste disposal.

Suitable Investment Ventures for Region X
Natural fibre production and processing, fruit/vegetable
production, rubber products and processing, industrial tree
production, coco oil mills, molasses production, sawmills,
plywood and veneer, hardwood, particles board manufacturing,
silica quartz, feldspar, white clay/ red clay manufacturing, and
wood-prying and processing

Southern Mindanao or Region XI

This consists of the provinces of Sarangani, South Cotabato, Davao
del Sur, Davao Oriental, Davao del Norte and Surigao del Sur.
Region XI is poised to become a leading growth pole of the country
with three prominent industrial zones: Ilang Agri-Industrial Estate
Corporation and Panacan Industrial Estate situated in Davao City
and Makar Industrial Estate in General Santos City.

The region is virtually typhoon-free with even rainfall and
temperatures throughout the year; hence it is blessed with vast
fertile lowlands critical for agro-based ventures. Southern
Mindanao is the Philippines' prime source of banana and pineapple
exports to Japan, the United States, Europe and the Middle East.
Aside from agri-based raw materials and products, metallic deposits
like gold, silver, copper, nickel, iron, chromate, magnesium as well

as non-metallic deposits like silica, limestone, shale, marble, sulphur, sand and clay are found in the provinces of the region.

All three dynamic industrial estates are conveniently located less than 10 km from the nearest airport and seaport. Besides the usual national incentives for industrial estates, Davao City provides additional perks. Such perks include exemption from the payment of certain local fees for priority investments in agri-business, tourism facilities, transhipment facilities, light manufacturing and property development.

The existing industries include Philippine-Japan Activated Carbon, Davao Union Cement Corporation, Davao Central Chemical Corporation, Bacnotan Consolidated Industries, Bandag Recapping Industries, DACEBU Exporters and Traders Corporation, Far East Cereals, Consolidated Plywood Corporation and Vitarich Corporation.

Suitable Investment Ventures for Region XI

Metalworking facilities, consumer products, feedmills, packaging plants, furniture and furnishing, food processing, gifts, toys, and household items

---

Central Mindanao or Region XII

This region, located at the mid-portion of mainland Mindanao, is blessed with a typhoon-free climate. Central Mindanao consists of three provinces—Lanao del Norte, Cotabato and Sultan Kudarat. Region XII is stretched over three geographical zones—the Lanao Lake area, the Cotabato River Basin area and the coastal areas in the north western and south western portions of the region. Copper and limestone are the major mineral reserves found in the region while non-metallic minerals are shale, silica and feldspar.

Growth in Central Mindanao will be boosted by the Iligan City Regional Industrial Centre in Linamon. The industrial centre is 26 km from the nearest airport and 16 km from the closest seaport. The Central Mindanao region has a well-developed road network that stretches to the remotest *barangays*. The Lake Lanao Agus River Complex provides the major source of power and has a total power output of 1,000 megawatts. Two river basins in Cotabato and Agusan supplement this hydro-electric power source.

Agro-industrial ventures suited for the Iligan City Regional Industrial Centre are integrated corn feed milling, integrated corn and cassava starch milling, integrated textile milling and garments manufacturing, integrated rice production and milling, banana production, fish processing, fruit production and processing, organic fertiliser production, and coffee processing.

Suitable Investment Ventures for Region XII

Rod and bar mills, steel services centre, foundry, electroplating plant, wire and nail manufacturing plant, bicycle and motorcycle production, porcelain insulator, car bodies and parts manufacturing, porcelain insulator making plant, woodscrew making plant, ceramic tableware making plant, wall tiles making plant, plastic container plant, concrete pole and pile plant, drycell plant, rigid PVC corrugated sheet making plant, industrial safety shoes/footwear production, and sanitary wares plant

---

The Autonomous Region of Muslim Mindanao (ARMM)
This region consists of Tawi-Tawi, Sulu, Maguindanao and Lanao del Sur. Major crops grown in the area include corn, coconut, *palay* (unhusked rice), banana, coffee, tobacco, mongo beans, cotton, cassava, rubber and legumes. The region is rich in natural resources and shows high potential for industrialisation.

The Parang Industrial Estate will be the hub of industrial activity in the ARMM. It lies 20 km from Cotabato City and the airport. The existing road network linking the province to the east (Cotabato and Davao) and to the south and south-east (Sultan Kudarat and South Cotabato) is well-developed.

Largely under-utilised, the lone modern seaport in Parang, Maguindanao Province is the Philippines' largest single port in the country. The port is 20 km north of Cotabato City and about 26 km from the Awang Airport.

Suitable Investment Ventures for ARMM

Fruit processing, organic fertiliser, corn, cassava starch and cassava chips, coconut milk, coffee processing, handicraft, wheat-flour mills, fish canning, board-box making, agricultural implements, coconut products manufacturing plant, soap and vinegar making, charcoal briquette, biscuit making, feedmills, and textile mills

---

Tourism Investments

Tourism is another sector that is benefiting tremendously from the Philippines' surging economy and stable political environment. Visitor arrivals for the past four years have been record-breaking, thereby increasing the demand for quality tourism enterprises.

Tourism is an important dollar-earner for the country. The government, therefore, seeks to spur the growth and development of this sector by providing fiscal incentives to prospective tourism investments. Additional incentives, especially for foreign investors, are remittance of earnings, repatriation of capital, right of succession, capital equipment incentives and income tax holidays. Tourism investment projects entitled to these incentives are tourism estates and ventures dealing in the development of tourist accommodation and transportation facilities.

Tourism Estates

A tourism estate involves the development of a large tract of land that is suitable for conversion into an integrated resort complex. It should have amenities similar to regular tourist facilities and activities, such as accommodation, food and beverage outlets, convention facilities, sports and, recreational centres, and commercial outlets. It should also have goad roads, water supply facilities, power supply, drainage and sewerage systems, and other necessary infrastructure. The estate must be located outside Metropolitan Manila and must provide the following facilities:

- Power transmission and/or distribution systems
- Main communication systems
- Water supply and distribution systems
- Sewerage and drainage extraction units
- Waste disposal systems
- Fire-fighting and fire prevention systems
- Basic medical clinic or hospital
- Convention facilities
- Security system

A number of priority sites have already been identified by the Philippine Department of Tourism as suitable locations for the establishment of pioneer tourist estates. These were selected because of their natural tourist endowments that blend in nicely with existing or proposed infrastructure (roads, bridges, ports, airports, water supply, electrical power and so forth). Local government officials and private citizens in these areas have also shown extraordinary commitment not only to their own tourism development also but to the country's overall tourism master plan.

A hot draw with tourists and investors is Baguio City, which has excellent potential for tourism development.

Samal Islands, Davao is located in the Gulf of Davao and is about 700 m south of Davao City. The total land area of the islands is around 28,000 hectares, of which Samal and Talikud Islands account for 95%.

Kaputian, the largest municipality with approximately 11,800 hectares of land and situated on the southern tip of Samal Islands, is now being developed into a major resort estate. The Samal Islands have the potential to house over 3,500 hotels, condominiums, apartments, villas and beach bungalows. Moreover, these can easily be supported by entertainment, sport, and food and beverage facilities.

Panglao Island, nestled between Bohol and Cebu, is connected by two bridges to Tagbilaran City, the provincial capital. The most notable attractions of Panglao are its white sandy beaches and excellent marine environment. In addition, the distinct culture of the inhabitants contributes to the island's unique character. The island could sustain a resort development of 3,000 rooms with scuba diving, marine sports as well as golf and other facilities.

Northern Palawan encompasses Puerto Princesa and the northward islands, including Cuyo, Cagayancillo and Balabac. The landscape is dramatic and breathtaking. It has pristine terrestrial and marine habitats, which are considered environmentally precious and ecologically fragile. Unlike other sites, Northern Palawan is not earmarked for the mass market due to environmental and socio-cultural reasons. As a special interest, low-volume and high-value destination, Northern Palawan promises to be an adventure of a lifetime for visitors and a source of considerable profit for investors.

Tagaytay City is located in the province of Cavite, which is a mere one-hour drive from Manila. It is often the first out-of-town destination for travellers. Tagaytay is perched on a mountain ridge 2,250 feet above sea-level, overlooking Taal Volcano. The city is the home of the Development Academy of the Philippines' modern seminar facilities. It also has picnic areas, a casino and sports facilities for swimming, horseback riding, tennis and racquetball. Moreover, Tagaytay's sound town planning, zoning and development have made it a well-organised city.

Taal Town has great potential as a tourism investment site. This may be attributed to the excellent preservation of Spanish and American colonial residences, churches and public structures. It is also located close to Tagaytay and the outlying towns of Batangas and Cavite. It is the launching pad for trips to Taal Volcano, one of the smallest active volcanoes in the world. All these pluses make the town a unique investment spot in southern Luzon.

Batangas Province is located on the south western part of Luzon. The whole province slopes north-west towards the coast. Most of Batangas was formed from rich volcanic ash that accumulated during the more active days of Taal Volcano thousands of years ago. Batangas has fine ports open to coastal trade and overseas shipping. It has an excellent land transportation infrastructure. Batangas offers many attractions like white sandy beaches, country clubs, reef clubs, parks, shrines, churches and historical landmarks.

Baguio City is nicknamed the summer capital of the Philippines and is located 5,000 ft above sea level on the ridges and plateaux of the Cordillera Mountain Range. Baguio City, the only city in the Province of Benguet, is 250 km north of Metro Manila. The city, with an area of 49 sq km of prime property, is highly urbanised. Baguio has a rugged and sloping terrain dotted with pine trees. It is approximately 50 minutes flying time from Manila. Loakan Airport in Baguio is about 20 minutes travel time by car south of the city. It is close to Fort Del Pilar where the Philippine Military Academy is located and is a scenic six-hour drive from Manila.

La Union is a well-known province located in north western Luzon. Its terrain is rugged, hilly and tightly squeezed between the mountains and the sea. In some places in the province, the sea laps at the foothills, creating magnificent beaches. The land is drained by the Amburayan River to the north and the Bauang River in the central region.

La Union is the primary administrative centre of the Ilocos region. The provincial capital, San Fernando, has an international seaport and offers great investment opportunities with proposed projects in infrastructure. It also has all-weather roads and major highways that link it with other provinces of northern Luzon.

Ilocos Sur is a historic province situated in the heartland of the Ilocos region. It is flanked by the South China Sea and the Cordillera Mountain Range. The sleepy, antiquated towns of the province are famous for their Catholic churches that take visitors back in time to the 19th century. The province is noted for its panoramic landscape and seascape. Vigan, the premier town of the province, has its own airport and boasts a number of centuries-old Spanish churches, public buildings and private residences.

Ilocos Norte is another historic province, which lies on the north western tip of Luzon overlooking the China Sea and the Balintang Channel. The terrain is formed by alluvial plains, hills, mountains, coasts and other land formations. The coastline, 140 km long, is dotted with coves and rivers. The province is known for its centuries-old historic spots, crystal clear coastal waters and miles of sandy beaches. Given the diversity of attractions in Ilocos Norte, the province's tourism potential is high. It is ideal for adventure travellers, scuba diving enthusiasts and seasoned travellers.

Boracay Island is located in the province of Aklan. Boracay has a total land area of approximately 1,000 hectares. The island is famous for "White Beach", which has been acclaimed as one of the best beaches in the world because of its white powdery sand. The island is lined by a long stretch of palm trees and crystal clear waters. Apart from this world-famous attraction, the island is also blessed with verdant hills, caves, forests, islets and coves. Areas that are opening up for investment include the development of a jetty port and improvements to Kalibo Airport's that would enable it to receive more and bigger aircraft. As for the beach, investors are needed in marina enhancement, water sports and games, and in in-camp site development.

Bicol Region or Bicolandia is a coastal area located in the southernmost tip of Luzon. Bicol is famous for Mayon Volcano, the most perfectly cone-shaped volcano in the world. Bicolandia is also popular for its beautiful beaches, thermal baths, old Spanish structures, pristine lakes, primeval forests and handcrafted products made of exotic fibres.

The Bicol Region has three major ports and caters to international and domestic shipping vessels. It is also accessible by air. Economic factors conducive to building a tourism estate—land, labour, capital and raw materials—are all abundant in this booming region. All it needs are the right entrepreneurs to blend together the essentials of a good investment.

Registration

The two basic documents required for the registration/administration of a tourism estate are an application form for registration under Executive Order 226 with the BOI and an endorsement from the Department of Tourism. Other supplementary paperwork to be submitted to the BOI and DOT are:

- A Land Conversion Clearance from the Department of Agrarian Reform
- A Locational Clearance from the Housing and Land Use Regulatory Board
- An Environmental Compliance Certificate from the Department of Environment and Natural Resources
- Other clearances/permits from local government agencies

Completion Requirement

The development of the proposed estate should be completed within a maximum of three years from the date of registration of the enterprise. Any slip in the implementation of the project shall be subject to penalty, including cancellation of the BOI registration.

Foreign ownership of the company developing or operating the tourism estate is allowed only if the project is granted pioneer status by the Department of Tourism.

Tourist Accommodation and Transportation Facilities

Aside from tourism estates, the Philippine Government encourages the establishment, expansion and modernisation of tourist accommodation facilities. As long as they are outside Metro Manila, such facilities as hotels, resorts, inns, pensiones and special interest resorts can be established.

Expansion projects shall be eligible for pioneer status if they involve the addition of guest rooms exceeding 25% of existing facilities for a deluxe or first-class-rated tourist facility. Expansion of facilities below the deluxe or first class or the equivalent shall be granted a non-pioneer status. Only expansions of tourist accommodation facilities outside Metro Manila are eligible for registration. A modernisation programme involves the upgrading of existing facilities to at least the class it is registered for with the Philippine Department of Tourism. Development of tourist transport facilities covers the operation of tour buses, as well as air and water transport.

The BOI and the Department of Tourism are the key government agencies for these projects. The DOT will have to give a favourabe endorsement of a tourism accommodation project to the BOI, which in turn will facilitate the setting up of the business venture. Interested overseas individuals can apply at the nearest Philippine diplomatic mission while those who are already in the Philippines can apply for a Special Investors Resident Visa (SIRV) directly at the DOT or the BOI's One-Stop-Action Centre.

CHAPTER 6

Management Matters

Foreigners doing business in the Philippines find a business climate that is a melting pot of North American, European and Asian influences. With the third largest English-speaking population in the world, a Catholic majority and an English-speaking media, the Philippines has a familiar feel for the Western business person. In fact, some have gone to the extent of describing the Philippines as a group of Latin American islands that drifted across the Pacific to Asia. Although the Philippine business culture is patterned on international models, the style and tone of business is much different from that prevalent in North America, Europe or even parts of Asia. As a result, knowledge of the local business culture and management practices is a must for the foreign business person.

This chapter seeks to provide an understanding of the business climate and management practices in the Philippines by discussing Filipino styles of management and leadership. It suggests ways of handling negotiations and conducting business in different social settings. It also touches on the role of women in business and society, business ethics, and office etiquette.

Filipino Management Style

Filipinos put high premium on persons in authority and, in general, identify leadership with benevolence.[1] Initiative is expected to come from above because the manager is considered the expert. At the same time, the manager acts as a parent for the employees. Not only does the manager ensure that they perform their tasks, he or she also has to be aware of their family life and personal problems that may affect job performance. The manager is expected to temper rules with consideration and justice with compassion and must always be careful not to offend and, of course, he or she must not take offence. The "hot button" must not be pressed unless a person's subjective core of self-worth is somehow touched. Appeals to subordinates must be shown or presented subjectively not distantly. Ideally, they must be preceded by personal contact.

Paternalistic leadership ("Work hard and the company will take care of you") appears to be the dominant leadership style among Filipino managers.[2] Paternalistic leaders expect everyone to work hard; in turn, they behave with a protective employee-centred concern.

Filipino employers place great emphasis on controlling their employees. They also show much concern for their welfare. They often treat their employees as strict but caring parents would their children. When poorly understood, however, this leadership approach can be misinterpreted as a leader having condescending confidence and trust in his or her subordinates.

Meetings

Compared to other Asians, Filipinos are less formal and more flexible in their business dealings. In general, Filipinos are accustomed to interacting with Americans and other Westerners. This makes the country a relatively easy place for Westerners to conduct business, albeit the massive traffic jams and other inconveniences associated with the infrastructure may prove irksome. Introductions are an important part of conducting business. Unless you work for a large, well-known multinational corporation, it is best to get an introduction from a representative, lawyer, consultant, banker or local partner.

Filipinos are impressed by titles and respect protocol. This has resulted in a proliferation of titles and job classifications in lieu of increases in salary. These act as motivators and boost job satisfaction without adding to the cost. Hence, when selecting a local partner or representative, it is important to ensure the person's credibility and "correct" political connections by probing into his or her existing clients as well as looking into his or her record.

Asia Money's Best Managed Philippine Companies (1996)	
Company	Rank
Manila Electric Company	1
Metro Bank	2
C&P Homes	3
Ayala Land	4
Piltel	5
Metro Pacific	6
Filinvest Land	7
SM Prime	7
Ayala Corporation	9
La Tondena	10
PLDT	10
San Miguel	10

Negotiations

Filipinos are more likely to trust you early on in your business relationship if you come with a favourable and credible introduction. They are also willing to spend time in developing personal relationships. The Filipino values *pakikisama* (smooth interpersonal relations). Given that getting along with a foreign business associate requires a great deal of time and effort, achieving *pakikisama*, which is a goal in itself, may even take precedence over accomplishing a specific task.

Frequent meetings, consultations and correspondences are necessary to establish and maintain a relationship. Due to the relative informal nature of Filipinos, it is not fruitful to be businesslike all the time. Common courtesies are all that are needed. Taboo conversation topics include religion, women, corruption and criticisms of the society. In business negotiations, every little detail, no matter how insignificant, should be discussed to avoid misunderstandings. Naturally, the price should be discussed last, after going through the basics of the deal. Generally, all decisions are made by people at the top of the hierarchy.

As prominent-sounding titles are abundant, make sure you are dealing with the correct level for decision-making. You must keep in mind that the person who makes the decisions for the Filipino negotiators is most likely not around in the room. Thus, pressing for a resolution before the parties leave the table is liable to accomplish little. It just makes everyone uncomfortable. Sometimes the foreigner is expected to take the initiative in the negotiations and aid his counterpart.

In the Philippines, the word "Yes" is indeterminate. It can mean "Yes, I agree," "Yes, I understand", "If that's what you want to hear", "Maybe", "Yes, I hope I sound unenthusiastic enough for you to

---

Affirmative Action?

Watch out—a Filipino may still say "Yes" or "Okay" to the boss even when:

- He is not sure of the boss' question.
- He wants to impress the boss but is really not quite clear on how to perform the task.
- He barely understood what the boss had said during the discussion or meeting.
- He is half-hearted about complying with the boss' instructions.
- He does not want to lose face in the presence of the boss or peers.
- He does not want the boss to lose face, especially in front of other people.
- He just wants to get it over with and move on to something more exciting to him.
- He is compelled by family pressure or honour to comply.

During a social get-together, you may come across a typical Filipino spread like the one above with a lechon or roast pig.

understand I really mean no" or "No, but I don't want to disappoint you or create a problem right now". You should confirm a "Yes" response several times and, in the case of a business agreement, eventually put it into writing.

Filipinos are non-confrontational, although not as reticent as the Japanese. Filipinos usually say "No" through a variety of creative ways, such as "I would like to, but I can't", "I would like to, but it is very difficult" and "I will try, and will let you know". To Filipinos, maintaining honour and saving face are very important. They dislike delivering bad news and often end up just saying nothing. Intermediaries may be used to raise issues that a Filipino may be embarrassed to address.

Filipinos have a reputation for being tough, capable and patient negotiators. Compared to other Asian countries, detailed legal contracts are easily drawn up in the Philippines and are honoured by business people.

Socialising

Filipinos believe that human interaction and contact form the basis of a successful business relationship. In the Philippines, who you know and who knows you are very important. Name-dropping is a normal way of getting to know people and is useful in establishing relationships. Personal relationships mean everything. Important matters cannot simply be handled by fax and telephone.

Business socialising is important to Filipinos. Business "power breakfasts" are common and often take place in hotel coffee shops. Business lunches are considered casual business meetings while business dinners or cocktails, considered more intimate, are usually reserved for a more mature stage in a developing relationship. A Filipino accepts a dinner invitation only if he or she feels comfortable around you. Generally, whoever extends the invitation pays for the meal. *Karaoke* or sing-along bars are popular in the Philippines. Here, your singing prowess is less important than your willing participation.

When Filipinos extend invitations to foreigners to visit their homes, this signifies acceptance. It is appropriate to bring flowers, a cake or a bottle of wine or liquor (unless the host is Muslim) when visiting a home. During dinner, the best compliment you can give your host is to eat the food heartily. Your willingness to try new food will gain you instant acceptance. You should always leave a portion of food on your plate to signify that you have finished eating.

Corruption

Traditionally, corruption has been part of Philippine business for some time. Although agent commissions are at the normal level, the agent may have additional costs related to securing the contract. These "third party commissions", known locally as *lagay*, can range from a couple of hundred dollars to thousands of dollars, depending on the size of the deal. It is wise to leave these matters to the local partner instead of handling them yourself. In most situations, it is not even necessary to take the wallet out of your pocket. When bribery occurs, it is usually done with inferiors and seldom with the decision-making company officers themselves. It is reasonable to make a distinction between the public and private sectors when talking about corruption. In the public sector, the roots of corruption are deep whereas in the private sector, competition is fairer. It is advisable to use a local representative who knows how to handle negotiations the Philippine way.

The government has, in recent years, addressed the problem of graft and corruption. The Hong Kong-based Political and Economic Risk Consultancy recently conducted a survey of 280 expatriate business executives, who ranked Asian countries on perceived corruption levels.[3] Of the 12 countries covered in the survey, only the Philippines and Singapore received better scores in 1997 compared to a 1996 survey. The Philippines has made a lot of progress in reducing the problem of corruption. This is a significant change from earlier years when it was regarded as one of Asia's most corrupt countries.

Office Etiquette

Business Hours   Most offices open their doors to the public between 8.00 a.m. and 10.00 a.m. Banks close at 3.00 or 3.30 p.m. while most offices and government authorities close at 5.00 p.m. Establishments usually have a five-day work week and there is normally a one-hour lunch break between noon and 2.00 p.m. Department stores are usually open from 9.00–9.30 a.m. to 7.00– 8.00 p.m. daily. Most private businesses are open seven days a week and close between 7.00 p.m. and 10.00 p.m. daily.

Punctuality   Foreigners' punctuality is appreciated, although Filipinos are traditionally late for every appointment, both professional and personal. When fixing a time for an appointment, one of the parties is likely to ask, "Is that Filipino or American time?" Filipino time generally means that the actual starting time will be 30 minutes to one hour later. Good-natured clarification of the intended time will lessen the foreigner's frustration. Fortunately, it is becoming less common among Filipinos to be late, particularly for business appointments. Nevertheless, the common Asian excuse of traffic jams and the weather during the rainy season will be accepted. You should leave plenty of time for travelling, especially to other parts of Metro Manila. You should not be surprised if the people you are meeting are late.

Dress Code By all accounts, Filipinos dress well and judge others by their dressing. Despite the warm weather, men should wear a suit to business meetings. In place of the jacket and tie, men could also wear the traditional open-necked *barong Tagalog* shirt, which is light, intricately embroidered and made of *jusi* (pineapple fibre). Wearing the *barong* indicates an interest in Philippine culture and customs, and gains the approval of Filipinos.

Women should wear a business suit (preferably a skirt and jacket) and—despite the heat—stockings. Filipinas tend to be more fashion conscious than other Asian women. However, modesty is always expected and appreciated. Foreign women are advised not to wear the local butterfly-sleeved dress or the *terno* as a business outfit. The dress is worn only on special occasions, such as fiestas or parades.

Business Cards and Gifts Business cards are useful at the first meeting. However, unlike elsewhere in Asia, Filipino do not consider it a failure if you do not have your business card at hand during the first meeting. The business card is a handy reference and it could be exchanged at the end of the meeting.

A foreign business person who decides to give a gift might consider one that is associated with his or her company (for example, pens or items with the company logo) or home country.

Traditional finery on display, with the man in a barong and the woman in a terno. Men may also wear the barong instead of a suit to business meetings

Other appropriate gifts include foreign liquor (provided the recipient is not a Muslim) or subscriptions to English-language business magazines. Do not open gifts in front of the person who gives it to you or in public. To do so indicates a materialistic nature on your part and may cause embarrassment to all parties present.

The Role of Filipino Women in Business and Society

Women have always enjoyed equality in Philippine society. Using measures of the relative empowerment of women in economic and political spheres of activity, the Philippines outperforms other Southeast Asian countries in gender equality in political, economic and professional activity.[4]

President Corazon C. Aquino is often used as an example of what women can accomplish in Philippine society. The appearance of women in important positions, however, is not new or even unusual in the Philippines. Filipinas have been senators, cabinet officers, supreme court justices, administrators and heads of major business enterprises for some time now. Women account for about a quarter (24%) of government officials and workers—the highest proportion in Southeast Asia—as well as 11.5% of legislative seats and one-third (33.7%) of administrators and managers. Since the early 1990s, women have been represented in many professions, although they predominate in domestic service (91%), professional and technical positions (62.7%) and clerical and sales (63%). Women are also often preferred in assembly-type factory work.

Other employment opportunities for women compare favourably with those open to men. This favourable occupational distribution does not mean that women do not at all face discrimination. Although they are eligible for high-level career positions, these are more often held by men. In 1990, women represented 64% of graduate students, but held only 159 of 982 top-level executive positions in the civil service. In the private sector, only about 15% of top-level positions were held by women.

Since the Spanish colonial period, women have been the family treasurer, which at least to some degree gave them the power of the purse. Nevertheless, the Spaniards also established a tradition of subordinating women, which is manifested in the latter's generally submissive attitudes. Male dominance has also been challenged, to some extent, in the Philippine Constitution of 1987. The Constitution contains an equal rights clause, although it lacks specific provisions that might make that clause effective.

Divorce is prohibited in the Philippines. In some circumstances, legal separation is permitted, but legal remarriage is not possible. The Family Code of 1988 is somewhat more liberal. Reflective of Roman Catholic Church law, the code allows annulment for reasons such as the following: psychological incapacity to be a marital partner, repeated physical violence against a mate or pressure by one mate to change the religious or political affiliation of the other. Divorce obtained abroad by a foreign spouse is also recognised. Although the restrictive divorce laws might be viewed as an infringement on a woman's right to get out of a bad marriage, indications are that many Filipinas view them as a protection against abandonment and loss of support by wayward husbands.

CHAPTER 7

Culture, Customs and Communication

The Philippines has over 50 ethnic groups, with Filipinos of Malay racial stock accounting for more than 95% of the population. Other significant influences in the racial composition are Indonesian and Chinese. The American, Arab, Indian, Negrito and Spanish influences are also present, though only marginally. Filipino culture itself is a mixture of Malay, Chinese, Spanish and American influences, with the country's citizens being invariably described as Malay in temperament, Chinese in filial piety, Spanish in gentility and American in ambition.[1]

Until recently, everything foreign has been much appreciated in the Philippines. Although its economic development has led to a healthy sense of nationalism, imported products still remain highly valued by the average consumer. This chapter outlines the relevant aspects of Filipino society by providing information about its cultural value orientations, social organisation, languages, religious life, education and communication patterns.

Filipino Cultural Values

The great majority of the population is bound together by common values and religion. Optimism and tolerance are typical features of the Filipino society and business culture. Power distance is high in the Filipino culture and is among the highest in the world's cultures.[2] As in Latin cultures generally, masculinity is of great importance. Family ties are strong and can even affect businesses. The high respect given to age should be taken into account when choosing representatives in the Philippines.

Philippine society is characterised by many positive traits. Among these are respect for authority, high regard for *amor proprio* (sensitivity to personal affront), strong religious faith and smooth interpersonal relationships. Filipinos' respect for authority is based on the special honour paid to elder members of the family and, by extension, to anyone in a position of power. This characteristic is generally conducive to the smooth running of the society although when abused, it can then develop into an authoritarianism that discourages independent judgement, individual responsibility and initiative.

Other values attributed to Filipinos include high standards of neatness and cleanliness maintained in personal grooming and in the home, and in many cases, despite limited budgets.[3] On the negative side, several writers mention the *mañana* habit (procrastination), *ningas kugon* or over-enthusiasm at the start of a project followed by a rapid loss of interest to the point where no work is completed, *pikon* (poor sportsmanship), "levelling" or the tendency to "bring down" through gossip those who rise above others in achievement, and colonial mentality or a penchant for imported goods and apathy towards one's own ideas.

Filipinos are also among the most hospitable people in the world. It is not uncommon, for example, for an overnight guest to be assigned the master bedroom. The fact that everybody speaks English makes it easy to feel comfortable among Filipinos. However, this might sometimes give rise to mistaken feelings of security and trust.

Filipinos are sensitive to attacks on their own self-esteem and are also sensitive to the self-esteem of others. Avoid saying or doing anything that may hurt a Filipino's self-esteem or you risk terminating the relationship. A person who is insensitive to others is said to lack a sense of shame and embarrassment, the principal sanction against improper behaviour. This great concern for self-esteem helps to maintain harmony in society and within one's particular circle but it can give rise to clannish behaviour and a willingness to sacrifice personal integrity to remain in the good graces of the group. Strong personal faith enables Filipinos face great difficulties and unpredictable risks in the assurance that "God will take care of things". But, if allowed to deteriorate into fatalism (locally known as the *bahala na* attitude), even this admirable characteristic can hinder initiative and stand in the way of progress.

Interpersonal Relations

Kinship
Interpersonal relations generally follow a single pattern, although variations do occur. These reflect the influence of local traditions. Among lowland Christian Filipinos, social organisation continues to be marked primarily by personal alliance systems, that is, groupings composed of kin (real and ritual), grantors and recipients of favours, and friends and partners in commercial exchanges.

Personal alliance systems are anchored by kinship, beginning with the nuclear family. Essentially, Filipinos' loyalty is with the immediate family; identity is deeply embedded in the web of kinship. It is the norm that one owes support, loyalty and trust to one's close kin, and because kinship is structured bilaterally with affinal as well as consanguineal relatives, one's kin can include quite a large number of people.

Beyond the nuclear family, Filipinos do not bestow the same degree of support, loyalty and trust that they do for immediate family members, for whom loyalty is nothing less than a social imperative. With regard to kin beyond this nuclear family, closeness in relationships depends very much on physical proximity.

Bonds of ritual kinship, sealed on any of the three ceremonial occasions—baptism, confirmation and marriage—intensify and extend personal alliances. This mutual kinship system, known as *compadrazo*, meaning "godparenthood" or sponsorship, dates back to the introduction of Christianity in the Philippines. It is a primary method of extending the group from which one can expect help in the way of favours, such as jobs, loans or just simple gifts on special occasions.

In asking a friend to the godparent of a child, a Filipino is also asking that person to become a closer friend. Thus, it is common to ask acquaintances who are of higher economic or social status to be sponsors. Such ritual kinship cannot be depended on in moments of crisis to the same extent as real kinship but it still functions for small and regular acts of support like gift giving.

Utang na loob Relationships

A dyadic bond—one between two individuals—may be formed based on the concept of *utang na loob* (debt of gratitude). Although it is expected that the debtor will attempt repayment, it is widely recognised that the debt (as in one's obligation to a parent) can never be fully repaid. The obligation can last for generations. Saving another's life, providing employment or making it possible for another to become educated are "gifts" that incur *utang na loob*. Moreover, such gifts initiate a long-term reciprocal interdependency in which the grantor of the favour can expect help from the debtor whenever the need arises and the debtor can, in turn, demand other favours.

Such reciprocal personal alliances have had obvious implications for the society in general and the political system in particular. Educated Filipinos are less likely to feel obligated to extend help (thereby not initiating an *utang na loob* relationship) compared to rural dwellers, among whom traditional values remain strong. Some observers believe that as Philippine society becomes more modernised and urbanised, *utang na loob* will become less important in the political and social systems.

Suki Relationships

In the commercial context, *suki* relationships (market-exchange partnerships) may develop between two people who agree to maintain a regular customer-supplier relationship. In the market place, Filipinos will regularly buy from certain specific suppliers who will give them, in return, reduced prices, good quality goods and often, credit.

Suki relationships often apply in other contexts as well. For example, regular patrons of restaurants and small neighbourhood retail and tailoring shops often receive special treatment in return for their patronage. The maintenance of these mutually beneficial supplier-customer relationships is one characteristic of Philippine business that makes it conducive for companies to implement a Total Quality Management philosophy. *Suki* does more than help develop economic exchange relationships. Trust creates a platform for a personal relationship, which can blossom into a genuine friendship between individuals.

Patron-client Bonds

Patron-client bonds are also very much a part of prescribed patterns of appropriate behaviour. These may be formed between tenant farmers and their landlords or between any patron who provides resources and influence in return for the client's personal services and general support.

The reciprocal arrangement typically involves the patron giving aid or employment, protection and influence and the client giving labour and personal favours, ranging from household tasks to political support. These relationships often evolve into ritual kinship ties as the tenant or worker may ask the landlord to be his or her child's godparent. Similarly, when favours are extended, they tend to bind a patron and client together in a network of mutual obligation or long-term interdependency.

Friendships

Filipinos also extend the circle of social alliances to friendship. Friendship is often placed on par with kinship as the most central

Major Philippine Cultural Festivals

New Year's Day	1 January (National Holiday)
Feast of the Black Nazarene	9 January (Quiapo, Manila)
Baguio Summer Festival	March (Baguio City)
Moriones Festival	March (Marinduque Province)
Holy Week	March or April (National Holiday)
Sinulog Festival	25 March (Ilog, Negros Occidental)
Labour Day	1 May (National Holiday)
Carabao Festival	14–15 May (Bulacan, Nueva Ecija and Rizal Provinces)
Pahiyas Festival	15 May (Quezon Province)
Flores de Mayo and Santacruzan Festivals	1–30 May
Independence Day	12 June (National Holiday)
Filipino-American Friendship Day	4 July (National Holiday)
Penafrancia Festival	September (Naga, Camarines Sur)
All Saints Day	1 November (National Holiday)
All Souls Day	2 November
Grand Canao	28 November–2 December (Baguio City)
Lantern Festival	24 December (San Fernando, Pampanga)
Christmas Day	25 December (National Holiday)
Rizal Day	30 December (National Holiday)

of Filipino relationships. Certainly ties among one's group of friends are an important factor in the development of personal alliance systems. Here, as in other categories, a willingness to help another provides the prime rationale for the relationship.

The categories—real kinship, ritual kinship, *utang na loob* relationships, *suki*-relationships, patron-client bonds and friendship—are not exclusive. They are interrelated components of the Filipino's personal alliance system. Thus, two individuals may be distant cousins, become friends and then cement their friendship through "godparenthood". Each of their social networks will typically include kin (near and far, affinal and consanguineal), ritual kin, one or two patron-client relationships, one or more other close friends (and a larger number of social friends), and a dozen or more market-exchange partners. *Utang na loob* may infuse any or all of these relationships. One's network of social allies may include 80 or more people, integrated and interwoven into a personal alliance system.

Social Organisation

Social Patterns

Filipino personal alliance systems extend far beyond the local arena, becoming pyramidal structures that extend all the way to Manila, where members of the national political elite represent the top of numerous personal alliance pyramids. Philippine elite comprises wealthy landlords, financiers, business people, high military officers and national political figures. Made up of a few families often descended from the *ilustrados* (wealthy Filipinos of Spanish lineage) or enlightened ones of the Spanish colonial period, the elite control a high percentage of the nation's wealth.

The lavish lifestyles of this group usually include owning at least two houses (one in Manila and one in the province where the family originated), patronising expensive shops and restaurants, belonging to exclusive clubs, and having a retinue of servants. Many count among their social acquaintances a number of rich and influential foreigners, especially Americans, Spaniards and other Europeans. Their children attend exclusive private schools in Manila and are often sent abroad, usually to the United States for higher education. Recently, a new elite group of business people, many from Hong Kong and Taiwan, has emerged in the urban areas.

In the cities, you can find a middle-class consisting of small entrepreneurs, civil servants, teachers, merchants, small property owners and clerks. These people have relatively secure jobs. In many middle-class families, both spouses work. They tend to place great value on higher education and most have a college degree. They also share a sense of common identity derived from similar educational experiences, facility in using English, common participation in service clubs like the Rotary and a similar economic standing.

Different income groups live in different neighbourhoods in the cities and lack the personal contact essential to the patron-client relationship. The major social division is probably between those with a regular source of income and those without one. The latter subsist by salvaging material from garbage dumps, begging, occasional paid labour and peddling. Although their income is sometimes as high as those in regular jobs, they lack the protection of labour legislation and have no claim to social insurance.

Urbanisation

By the year 2000, it is forecasted that the majority (59%) of Filipinos will live in urban areas. The Philippines, like most other Southeast Asian nations, has one dominant city that is in a category all by itself as a "primate city" (a major city).

Metro Manila, with a population of 9.28 million in 1995, produces roughly half of the Philippines' GNP and contains two-thirds of the nation's vehicles. Its plethora of wholesale and retail business establishments, insurance companies, advertising companies and banks of every description makes the region the unchallenged hub of business and finance.

Metro Manila has some of the best colleges and universities in Southeast Asia, such as the University of the Philippines, Ateneo de Manila University and De La Salle University. The Metro Manila area is thus a magnet for the best minds of the nation.

In addition to being the political and judicial capital, Manila is also the entertainment and arts capital, with all the glamour of first-class international hotels and restaurants. As the capital dominates the communications and media industry, Filipinos everywhere are constantly made aware of the economic, cultural and political events in Manila. Large numbers of rural Filipinos move to the city in search of economic and other opportunities. More than half the residents of Metro Manila are born elsewhere.

Manila, especially the Makati section, has a modern superstructure of hotels, banks, supermarkets, malls, art galleries and museums. Beneath this structure, however, is a substructure of traditional small neighbourhoods and a wide spectrum of lifestyles ranging from traditional to modern, and from those of the inordinately wealthy to those of the abjectly poor.

Metro Manila has greater economic extremes than other urban areas. In the latter, poverty is clearly visible from the thousands of flimsy squatter shacks dotting the landscape. These shacks contrast with the elegant, guarded suburbs that house expensive homes and private clubs. In Manila, however, these economic divisions are not paralleled by residential patterns based on racial background or region of origin. Manila and other Philippine cities are truly melting pots, in which wealth is not the only determinant of residence.

Whether in poor squatter and slum communities or in the middle-class sections of cities, values associated primarily with rural *barangays* continue to be important in determining expectations and actions. Even when it is clearly impossible to create a warm and personal community in a city neighbourhood,

Filipinos nevertheless feel that traditional patterns of behaviour conducive to such a community should be followed. Hospitality, interdependence, patron-client bonds and real kinship continue to be of importance to urban Filipinos.

Still another indication that traditional Philippine values remain functional for city dwellers is the average household size, which is greater in urban than rural areas. As Filipinos move to the cities, they tend to have fewer children but they more than make up for it by having more extended family members and non-relatives in their households.

This situation might have been caused by such factors as the availability of more work opportunities in the city, the tendency of urban Filipinos to marry later resulting in more singles, the housing industry's inability to keep pace with urbanisation and the high urban unemployment rates that cause families to supplement their incomes by taking in boarders. Whatever the reason, it seems clear that kinship and possibly other personal alliance system ties are no weaker for most urban Filipinos than they are for their rural counterparts.

Poverty

During the period 1989–1994, about 41% of the population lived below the poverty line, a decline from more than half in 1985. The countryside contains a disproportionate share of the poor. For example, more than three quarters of the poorest 30% of families live in the rural areas. The majority are tenant farmers or landless agricultural workers. The landless, fishermen and forestry workers are found to be the poorest of the poor. Some rural regions, the most obvious example being the sugar-growing region on the island of Negros, occasionally experience famine. Many people here suffer from malnutrition.

The Ifugao tribe at the Grand Canao festival in Baguio City. There are over 50 ethnic minorities in the Philippines, a reflection of the country's cultural diversity.

The urban poor generally live in crowded slum areas, often on land or in buildings without the permission of the owners; hence they are referred to as "squatters". These settlements often lack basic necessities like running water, sewage facilities and electricity. According to a 1984 government study, 44% of all occupied dwellings in Metro Manila had less than 30 sq m of living area and the average monthly expenditure of an urban poor family was PHP1,315 (about US$80, based on the 1984 exchange rate). Of this, 62% was spent on food and another 9% on transportation, whereas only PHP57 (about US$3.40) was spent on rent or mortgage payments because of the extent of squatting by poor urban families.

About 55% of the poor surveyed in the labour force worked in the informal sector, generally as vendors or street hawkers. Other activities included service and repair work, construction, transport services or petty production. Women and children under 15 years of age constituted almost 60% of those employed. The majority of individuals surveyed possessed a high school education and 30% possessed skills like dressmaking, electrical repair, plumbing or carpentry. Nevertheless, they were unable to secure permanent, full-time positions.

Urban squatters have been a perennial problem or perhaps, a symptom of a problem. Large numbers of people living in makeshift housing, often without water or sewage, indicate that cities have grown in population faster than the required facilities. In fact, the growth in population even exceeds the demand for labour. Many squatters make a living by salvaging materials from garbage dumps, peddling and performing irregular day work.

Most squatters are long-time residents, who find not having to pay rent a way of coping with economic problems. Recent government efforts to beautify and modernise the Metro Manila area have inevitably led to conflicts with the squatters, who have settled on most of the land that could be utilised in such projects. The forced eviction of squatters and the destruction of their shacks are frequent occurrences. Both the authoritarian Marcos government and the democratic Aquino and Ramos governments have found it hard to handle the squatter problem. All proposed solutions contained difficulties. Probably, only a major economic recovery in the rural and urban areas would provide a setting in which a degree of success would seem possible.

The growth of other urban centres in the late 1980s and early 1990s has signalled a slowdown in the expansion of Metro Manila. The average growth rate of Metro Manila slowed down from 6.9% (1970–1975) to 3.1% (1990–1995). This situation has been caused, at least in part, by the policies of the Marcos, Aquino and Ramos governments. The Marcos administration encouraged industrial decentralisation and prohibited the erection of new factories within 50 km of Manila.

In an effort to relieve unemployment, the Aquino and Ramos administrations spent billions of pesos on rural infrastructure, which helped expand business to the nearby cities. Cities such as Iligan, Cagayan de Oro and General Santos on Mindanao and, especially Cebu on Cebu Island have experienced economic growth in the 1980s far exceeding that of Metro Manila.

Languages

The official languages are English and Pilipino, with English as the language of the government, commerce and media. There are 168 languages and dialects spoken in the Philippines.[4] Of these, nine are the mother tongues of about 88% of Filipinos.

The nine most widely spoken native languages, in decreasing frequency, are Tagalog, Cebuano, Ilocano, Hiligaynon, Bicolano, Waray-Waray, Pampangan, Pangasinan and Magindanaon. All nine belong to the Malayo-Polynesian language family and are related to Bahasa Indonesia and Bahasa Melayu, although no two are mutually comprehensible. Each language has a number of dialects and all have impressive literary traditions, especially Tagalog, Cebuano and Ilocano.

Tagalog is the principal base of Pilipino, the national language. Although Tagalog is the mother tongue of only 24% of Filipinos, the majority can speak Pilipino in varying degrees of fluency. Some languages have closer affinity with one another than with others. For example, it is easier for Ilocanos and Pangasinans to learn each other's language than to learn any of the other seven major languages. Likewise, speakers of the major Visayan languages— Cebuano, Hiligaynon, and Waray-Waray—find it easier to communicate with one another than with speakers of Tagalog, Ilocano or the other languages.

Nowhere are language divisions more apparent than in the continuing public debate over the national language. The

The religious fervour of the flagellants during the Lenten period in March and April. Religion is a major influence on Filipinos, most of whom are Roman Catholic.

government in 1974 initiated a policy of gradually phasing out English in schools, business and government, and replacing it with Pilipino, based on the Tagalog language of Central and Southern Luzon. Pilipino had by then spread throughout the nation, affecting the mass media and the school system. In 1990, President Corazon C. Aquino ordered that all government offices use Pilipino as a medium of communication. Some 200 college executives asked that Pilipino be the main medium of college instruction rather than English. Government and educational leaders hoped that Pilipino would be in general use by the end of the century. By that time, it might have enough grassroots support in non-Tagalog-speaking regions to become a national language. Today, however, Filipinos still have not accepted a national language at the expense of their regional languages. There is also no agreement on whether regional languages should be subordinated to a national language based on Tagalog.

There has been much debate on the role of English in the Philippines. Some argue that English is essential to economic progress because it opens up the country to the rest of the world, facilitates foreign commerce and makes Filipinos desirable workers for international firms both in the Philippines and abroad.

Despite figures that show that nearly 65% of the population claim some understanding of English, there is growing concern that competence in English has deteriorated in recent years. There are debates over whether "Filipinisation" and the shift of the language towards "Taglish" (a mixture of Tagalog and English) have made it less useful as a medium of international communication. However, major newspapers are in English, English language movies are popular and English is the language often used in print advertisements.

Successful Filipinos are likely to continue to be competent in both Pilipino and English. Speakers of another regional language would most likely continue using that language at home, Pilipino in ordinary conversation in the cities and English for commerce, government and international relations. Both Pilipino, which is gaining use in the media, and English continue to be the languages of education.

Religious Life
Religion holds a central place in the life of most Filipinos. The religious composition remains predominantly Christian. Approximately 83% of the population are Roman Catholics while Protestants account for 6%. The main religious minorities are Muslims (5% of the population) and Buddhists (less than 1% of the population).

Religion is central to Filipinos not as an abstract belief system but rather as a host of experiences, rituals, ceremonies and special occasions that provide continuity in life, cohesion in the community and moral purpose for existence. Religious associations are part of the system of kinship ties, patron-client bonds and other links outside the nuclear family.

Christianity and Islam have been superimposed on ancient traditions and culture. Unique religious blends and the combination of the strong personal faith of Filipinos have given rise to many diverse revivalist movements. Many have been swept up in such movements as *El Shaddai* out of a renewed sense of fraternity and community.

Like the highly visible examples of flagellation and re-enacted crucifixion in the Philippines, these movements may seem to have little in common with organised Christianity or Islam. However in the intensely personalistic Filipino religious context, they have not been aberrations as much as extreme examples of how religion retains its central role in society.

Christians are found throughout the archipelago. There are also a small number of Buddhists, Taoists and tribal animists. Muslims remain largely in the south and are less integrated into mainstream Philippine culture than other religious minorities.

Although most Chinese are members of Christian churches, a minority of Chinese worship in Taoist or in Buddhist temples, the most spectacular of which is an elaborate Taoist temple on the outskirts of Cebu City.

Education

The educational system offers six years of elementary instruction followed by four years of high school. Children enter primary school at the age of seven. Instruction is bilingual in Pilipino and English, although it is often claimed that the former is favoured over the latter. Before independence in 1946, instruction in schools was completely in English. Since then the national language, Pilipino, has been increasingly emphasised.

Until the compulsory study of Spanish was abolished in 1987, secondary school students as well as tertiary level students had to contend with three languages—Pilipino, English, and Spanish. The Department of Education, Culture and Sports is solely responsible for education. It has direct supervision over public schools and sets mandatory policies for private schools as well.

The Philippines has an adult literacy rate of 95%. Among the East Asian countries, only Japan and South Korea have higher literacy rates. Elementary education is compulsory and free for six years. In 1989, around 15 million students benefited from this. In the same year, approximately 290,000 teachers were employed in 34,000 elementary schools across the country.

Children enrol in secondary schools at age 13. In 1989, there were approximately four million students enrolled in 5,500 secondary schools with approximately 80,000 teachers. That year, another 1.6 million were enrolled in 1,675 institutions of higher learning with 56,380 instructors. In 1994, 78% of Filipinos in the 6–23 age group were enrolled in institutions of learning, an increase from 61% in 1980. This gross enrolment ratio is the highest among the Southeast Asian countries.

There have been significant differences in literacy for different regions of the country and between rural and urban areas. The Western Mindanao Region, for example, has a literacy rate of 65% as compared with 90% for Central Luzon and 95% for Metro Manila. Due to the country's industrialisation efforts, vocational education has received greater emphasis. Traditionally, however, Filipinos have tended to equate the attainment of education directly with escape from manual labour. Hence, it has not been easy to win general support for vocational training.

Catholic and Protestant churches sponsor schools. There are also proprietary (privately owned, non-sectarian) schools. Neither the proprietary nor the religious schools receive government support, except occasional subsidies for special programmes. Only about 6% of elementary students are in private schools, but this rises sharply to about 63% at the secondary level and about 85% at the tertiary level. About a third of the private school tertiary-level enrolment is in religious-affiliated schools.

In 1990, over 10,000 foreign students studied in the Philippines, mostly in the regular system. There are three main schools for international students—Brent School (Baguio City), and Faith Academy and the International School (Manila). These schools have some Filipino students and faculty members, but the majority are foreigners, mostly American. Faith Academy serves primarily the children of missionaries, although others are also admitted subject to availability of space.

The Chinese have established their own system of elementary and secondary schools. On a typical day, classes in the morning cover the usual Filipino curriculum and are taught by Filipino teachers. In the afternoon, classes are taught by Chinese teachers and offer instruction in Chinese language and literature.

A serious problem for the Philippines concerns the large number of students who complete college but are not able to find a job commensurate with their educational skills. If properly utilised, these trained personnel could facilitate economic development, but when left idle or forced to take on jobs for which they are over-qualified, they could be a major source of discontent. During the past 20 years, these unemployed or under-employed graduates have served as the backbone of the country's overseas contract workforce.

Body Language, Gestures and Greetings

The Philippines is a high context culture, that is, one in which the circumstances, tone and manner of speech are liable to be as important as the words spoken.

A variety of body language moves exists in Filipino culture. Filipinos often greet each other with slightly raised eyebrows or a small nod of the head as if to signal recognition. This body language is often accompanied by a smile, signifying a friendly "Hello". Filipinos do not speak in a belligerent, harsh or loud manner, nor do they stare. These are considered rude behaviour. Standing with your hands on your hips is interpreted as anger or a confrontational pose.

Filipinos tend to smile in a range of circumstances, even to cover up discomfort, sadness or nervousness. Filipinos rarely frown and smiles are an important part of their culture. Filipinos appreciate a good sense of humour and enjoy telling jokes. Close friends will often make jokes at each other's expense and everyone generally accepts such bantering from time to time.

When beckoning someone, do not point at the person nor beckon with just the index finger. You should use the whole hand with the palm facing down and fingers pointing away, but moving toward you in a scratching motion. Filipinos also point by pouting their mouth in the direction indicated or by moving their eyes to the relevant direction.

Compared with other Asians, Filipinos tend to be more physical. Do not be alarmed by a pat on your back by a Filipino. It is best not to initiate such gestures. In fact, a man should not initiate a handshake with a woman, although he may follow through if she extends her hands. Physical contact in public may exist between people of the same gender, but never with someone of the opposite gender.

Filipino business people usually greet each other with a handshake and a friendly smile. Filipinos are respectful of all, regardless of rank, so there is usually no distinction in address based on superior-subordinate relationships. However, Filipinos generally address superiors with the English "Sir" or "Ma'am" in both business and social circles and are generally uncomfortable with a more informal approach.

After a closer relationship develops, it becomes more natural to use first names but you should generally wait until you have been invited to do so. In business meetings or in other formal settings, people are often referred to by their occupational or professional titles—for example, Dr Santos, Attorney Castillo, Engineer Braga, Architect Ragasa or Professor Reyes. In the Philippines, the foreign business person can never be too respectful, regardless of status.

Useful Phrases

Most Filipinos are fluent in English so, there is little need for translation in normal business and social encounters. The most important Tagalog phrase is *Mabuhay* ("Long live", "Welcome" or "Greetings"), which is often used to toast someone. The following are some Tagalog phrases that foreigners may find useful:

Hello (informal)	*Kumusta [Coo-moose-TAH]*
Hello (formal)	*Kumusta po kayo [Coo-moose-TAH po kha-yo]*
My name is …	*Ako si …[A-KO-see …]*
Good morning	*Magandang umaga po*
	[Ma-GUN-dang oo-ma-GA po]
Good afternoon	*Magandang hapon po*
	[Ma-GUN-dang hap-PON po]
Good evening	*Magandang gabi po*
	[Ma-GUN-dang ga-BEE po]

Thank you	*Salamat po [Sah-la-MAT po]*
You are welcome	*Walang anuman po*
	[Wa-LUNG a-noo-MAN po]
Cheers	*Mabuhay [Mah-BOO-high]*
Good-bye	*Paalam na po [Pa-A-lam na po]*

Basic Facts and Travel Tips

Right in the heart of Southeast Asia is the Philippines, a long chain of some 7,107 islands and islets. From north to south, this tropical archipelago stretches for more than 1,700 km towards the Equator. The South China Sea washes its western shores. Its northern neighbours include Taiwan, Hong Kong and China. Further north is Japan. Westward lies other Southeast Asian countries like Thailand, Malaysia and Singapore. An arm of the archipelago points south-west towards the isle of Borneo and at its feet, is the island chain of Indonesia. To the east and south, the waters of the Pacific Ocean sweep its headlands, looking out towards Micronesia and Polynesia.

The total land area of the Philippines is 299,404 sq km. It has an irregular coastline that covers some 334,539 km. The current population is approximately 70 million. The country enjoys one of the highest literacy rates in Asia at 95%. Pilipino is the national language but English, Chinese and Spanish are also spoken by segments of the population. There are over 70 dialects of ethno-Malay origin. The Philippines is also one of the largest English-speaking countries in Southeast Asia. More than 85% of the population is Roman Catholic. The capital city is Manila.

The country is readily accessible from the capital cities of the world. Approximate travel times to Manila are as follows:

- Hong Kong (2 hours)
- Singapore (3 hours)
- Bangkok (3 hours)
- Tokyo (3 hours and 30 minutes)
- Sydney (10 hours and 20 minutes)
- London (20 hours and 45 minutes)
- Paris, 21 hours
- Frankfurt (19 hours and 40 minutes)
- San Francisco (20 hours and 15 minutes)
- Los Angeles (15 hours and 20 minutes)
- New York (25 hours and 20 minutes)

Accommodation

In Metro Manila and most large provinces, there is a wide selection of deluxe, standard and pensione-type accommodation. There are 7,708 hotel rooms in Metro Manila and 29,698 Department of Tourism-licensed hotel rooms throughout the country.

The Department of Tourism has a Homestay Programme in 15 destinations outside Manila. This programme offers visitors the comfort of modest homes and an insight into Philippine life. There are currently more than 200 homeowners accredited under this programme. Visitors interested in the Homestay Programme may contact the Tourist Information Centre located at the Gallery area, Department of Tourism Building, Tel: 523-8411/30.

Airports

Manila is served by the Ninoy Aquino International Airport (NAIAI), 7 km from the city centre and by the Manila Domestic Airport, which is 1 km from the NAIA. Cebu is served by the Mactan International Airport (MIA), which is 45 minutes from the city centre. Both international airports have adequate traveller facilites: duty-free shopping centres, souvenir shops, tourist information centres, hotel and travel agency representatives, and car rental services. The NAIA has banks, a postal service, medical clinic and a baggage deposit area.

Airport Fees

Ninoy Aquino International Airport: PHP500; Mactan International Airport: PHP500.

Airport Transfers

Car Rental

Limousine service by reputable car rental companies is available at NAIA. At the Mactan International Airport, a trip to the city by a hired car costs approximately PHP200. This is to be paid directly to the driver or at the designated counters in the airport.

Hotel Cars

Hotel transport can be arranged with hotel representatives at designated counters situated at the Arrival lobby of the NAIA and the Mactan International Airport.

Taxis

Avis operates the only accredited taxi service at the NAIA. Coupons are available at the Avis counter situated at the arrival lobby. At the Manila Domestic Airport, G&S is the authorised pre-paid coupon taxi company. Metered taxi rates in Cebu range from PHP60 to PHP70 from the airport to the city proper.

Business and Banking Hours

Private and government offices are open either from 8.00 a.m. to 5.00 p.m. or from 9.00 a.m. to 6.00 p.m., Mondays to Fridays. Some private companies are open on Saturdays from 9.00 a.m. to noon. Most shopping centres, department stores and supermarkets open from 10.00 a.m. to 8.00 p.m. daily. Banks are open from 9.00 a.m. to 3.00 p.m., Mondays to Fridays.

Climate

The months from March to May are hot and dry, with temperatures ranging from 22–32°C. The months from June to October are rainy while November through February are cool, with temperatures ranging from 22–28°C. Average humidity year-round is 77%.

Communications Facilities

International direct dialing, telex, facsimile, worldwide express delivery, postal services and telegraphic services are available in most major cities. Most newspapers and magazines are in English while the rest are in Pilipino or the various dialects. Foreign newspapers and magazines are sold at major hotels, supermarkets and bookstores in Metro Manila.

Credit Cards

International credit cards such as Visa, Diners Club, Bank-Americard, Mastercard and American Express are accepted in major establishments.

Currency Regulations

Visitors carrying more than US$3,000 are requested to declare the amount at the Central Bank of the Philippines counter situated at the customs area.

Foreign currency taken out upon departure must not exceed the amount brought in. Keep all exchange receipts for record purposes. Departing passengers may not bring out more than PHP5000 in local currency.

Customs Regulations

To facilitate customs examination, visitors are advised to fill in the Baggage and Currency Declaration Form before disembarking. Visitors are allowed to bring in the following articles duty-free: reasonable quantity of clothes, jewellery and toiletries, 400 sticks of cigarettes or two tins of tobacco, and two bottles of wine or spirits of not more than one litre each.

Domestic Transport

Air

Philippine Airlines provides daily services to and from 42 local destinations. Pacific Airways has scheduled and chartered flights to major domestic destinations. Other domestic airlines include Cebu Pacific and Air Philippines.

Land

Jeepneys and buses are inexpensive ways to get around. In Manila, air-conditioned buses ply certain key routes. Roofless double-decker buses run along Roxas Boulevard from Rizal Park. Metered taxis generally cruise for hire. The elevated Light Rail Transit (LRT) provides a fast, efficient rail system along a 15-km line from Baclaran in the south to Caloocan City in the north. There are 15 stations, spread 8-m apart, at major intersections. Travelling time from one end to another is 30 minutes.

The Metro Tren offers commuter train service from Espana Street in Muntilupa, a suburb south of Manila. The Metro Ferry plies the waters of the Pasig River from Escolta in Manila to Guadalupe in Makati. Cars and air-conditioned tourist buses are also available for hire from licensed tourist transport operators in major cities. Most hotels have limousine service.

Sea

Inter-island ships connect Manila to major ports. Ferry services connect the smaller islands. Departure schedules from the Port of Manila can be found in the local newspapers.

Drug Abuse

Possession or use of prohibited drugs carries a maximum penalty of imprisonment of 20 years and a fine of PHP20,000.

Duty-free Shopping

Duty-free shops are located at the departure and transit areas of NAIA and MIA in Cebu. There are also Duty-free outlets at the Manila Hotel, the Hotel Nikko Manila Garden and the Century Park Sheraton Hotel.

The Duty-free Fiesta Shopping Centre near the NAIA is the county's largest duty-free outlet. Overseas Filipinos returning to the Philippines under the "Balikbayan Plus" programme of the Department of Tourism have special duty-free shopping privileges.

Entry Regulations

Except for stateless persons and those from countries with which the Philippines has no diplomatic relations, all visitors with valid passports may enter the country without visas and may stay for 21 days provided they hold tickets for onward journeys. Holders of Hong Kong and Taiwan passports must have special permits. Visas and special permits may be obtained from Philippine embassies and consulates.

Getting There

Manila, Cebu and Davao are international gateway cities strategically located in the heart of trade and investment centres in Luzon, the Visayas and Mindanao respectively.

Manila is served by more than 30 airlines, which fly to different cities throughout the world. Philippine Airlines, the country's flag carrier, links Manila to 26 cities in 19 countries and plies the air routes of principal cities and towns all over the country. Aerolift has scheduled flights to Boracay in Aklan, Bagabag Airport in Banaue and Busuanga in Palawan.

Manila's air and sea ports bustle with the comings and goings of major international carriers and cruise liners. Cebu City handles regular flights from Japan, Singapore and Australia, as well as charter flights from Hong Kong, the United States and other major travel markets. Davao City likewise receives direct flights from Manila and Singapore. Subic Bay International Airport, Clark International Airport and Laoag International Airports are currently in the process of accepting increased international flights from countries within and outside the Asia-Pacific region.

Health Regulations

A certificate of vaccination against yellow fever is required for travellers coming from infected areas. Children below the age of one are subject to isolation when necessary.

Language

Pilipino is the national language although English, Spanish and Chinese are also used in business and government.

Metro Manila

Comprising four cities and 13 municipalities, Metro Manila is home to roughly 20% of the country's total population. Manila, the capital city is situated at the mouth of a natural harbour—the Manila Bay. Malacanang Palace, the official residence of the president, stands regally on the banks of the Pasig River.

Porterage
For passengers arriving at the NAIA, baggage carts are available for US$1. Porterage fee on departure is PHP5 per baggage. At the Mactan International Airport, porters are paid PHP2 per baggage.

Time Zone
GMT plus eight hours.

Tipping
Tipping is expected for many services. The standard amount is 10% of the total bill. Tipping is optional in most hotels and restaurants that already include a 10% service charge.

Tours and Special Interest Activities
Exciting tour packages, from day trips to five-day programmes provide glimpses of the country's diverse attractions. Special interest activities include golfing, game-fishing, water-skiing, diving, mountain climbing, trekking and safari trips. Fiesta and village tours, cultural and historical tours, and visits to farms and ancestral houses are also available.

Unit of Currency
Philippine Peso (PHP) = 100 centavos. Bank notes: PHP5, PHP10, PHP20, PHP50, PHP100, PHP500, PHP1000. Coins 1c, 5c, 10c, 25c, 50c, PHP1, PHP2, PHP5.

What to Wear
Light casual clothes are recommended. Warmer garments are needed for mountainous regions. During formal occasions, a dinner jacket and tie or the Philippine *barong Tagalog* may be worn.

Directory of Important Contacts

Trade and Investment One-Stop Action Centres

These centres provide facilities and services that enable the investor to obtain the necessary investment information and documentation from just one location.

**One-Stop Action Centre
for Investments**
Board of Investment (BOI)
Ground Floor, Industry
and Investment Building
385 Senator Gil J. Puyat Avenue
Makati City
Tel: (632) 895-8322/896-7342
Fax: (632) 895-3977/890-3051

**One-Stop Export Documentation
Centre**
International Trade
Centre Complex
Roxas Boulevard
Pasay City
Tel: (632) 831-1812
Fax: (632) 831-2201

**One-Stop Import
Processing Centre**
Department of Trade and Industry
Bureau of Import Services
Industry and Investment Building
385 Senator Gil J. Puyat Avenue
Makati City
Tel: (632) 890-4912
Fax: (632) 831-7252

**One-Stop Shop Tax
Credit Centre**
Department of Finance
CB Multi Storey Building
Roxas Boulevard, Manila
Tel: (632) 526-2293
Fax: (632) 527-4285, 527-4276

**One-Stop Action Garments
Export Assistance Centre**
Garments and Textile Export Board
3rd & 4th Floors
New Solid Building
357 Senator Gil Puyat Avenue
Makati City
Tel: (632) 890-4912
Fax: (632) 817-4974

The Twelve Biggest Law Firms Specialising in Philippine Business

Castillo Laman Tan Pantaleon & San Jose
2nd, 3rd & 4th Floors
The Valero Tower
122 Valero cor. Herrera Streets
Makati City
Tel: (632) 817-6791 to 95,
810-4371
Fax: (632) 819-2724 to 25,
817-5938
E-mail: counsel@cltpsj.com.ph

Sycip Salazar Hernandez & Gatmaitan
2nd-4th Floors,
Sycip All-Asia Law Centre
105 Paseo de Roxas, Makati City
Tel: (632) 817-9811 to 20
Fax: (632) 817-3896

Angara Abello Concepcion Regala & Cruz
5th Floor, ACCRA Building
122 Gamboa Street
Legaspi Village, Makati City
Tel: (632) 817-0966
Fax: (632) 816-0119

Platon Martinez Flores San Pedro & Leano
6th Floor Tuscan Building
Herrera Street
Legaspi Village, Makati City
Tel: (632) 867-4696
Fax: (632)967-1304
E-mail: lawfirm@webquest.com

Quisumbing Torres & Evangelista
11th Floor, Pacific Star Building
Makati Avenue corner
Senator Gil Puyat
Makati City
Tel: (632) 817-3016, 811-5925,
815-2091
Fax: (632) 817-4432, 817-5416

Ponce Enrile Cayetano Reyes & Manalastas
3rd Floor Vernida IV Building
Alfaro Street, Salcedo Village
Makati City
Tel: (632) 815-9571
Fax: (632) 818-7355

Romulo Mabanta Sayoc Buenaventura & De Los Angeles
30th Floor
Citibank Tower
8741 Paseo de Roxas
Salcedo Village
Makati City
Tel: (632) 848-0114
Fax: (632) 815-3172

Bengzon, Narciso, Cudala, Pecson, Bengson & Jimenez
16th Floor,
Sol Building
112 Amorsolo Street
Legaspi Village
Makati City 1229
Tel: (632) 815-9071
Fax: (632) 817-3251

Ledesma Saludo & Agpalo
4th Floor, Parkview Building
112 Gamboa Street,
Legaspi Village
Makati City
Tel: (632) 892-1596
Fax: (632) 810-7379

Bito Lozada Ortega & Castillo
5th & 6th Floors, Akpap I Building
140 Alfaro Street, Salcedo Village
Makati City
Tel: (632) 818-2321
Fax: (632) 810-3153

**Siguion Reyna Montecillo
& Ongsiako**
9th & 10 Floors,
Philcomcen Building
8755 Paseo de Roxas
Makati City 1200
Tel: (632) 810-0281 to 90,
810-0409
Fax: (632) 819-1498

Carag Caballes Jamora & Somera
2nd Floor Plaza Royal
120 Alfaro Street, Salcedo Village
Makati City
Tel: (632) 812-5246
Fax: (632) 818-8971

Important Agencies at the Government Level

Board of Investments (BOI)
Industry & Investment Building
385 Senator Gil Puyat Avenue
Makati City
Tel: (632) 890-1332, 897-6682

**Bureau of Export
Trade Promotion (BETP)**
6/F New Solid Building.
357 Senator Gil Puyat Avenue
Makati City
Tel/Fax: (632) 817-2803, 890-5203

Bureau of Food and Drug (BFD)
Alabang, Muntinlupa
Tel/Fax: (632) 842-5635

Bureau of Immigration
Magallanes Drive, Intramuros
Metro Manila
Tel/Fax: (632) 527-3265

Bureau of Internal Revenue (BIR)
BIR Building, East Triangle
Diliman, Quezon City
Tel: (632) 929-7676

Bureau of Mines & Geo-Sciences
North Avenue, Diliman
Quezon City
Tel/Fax: (632) 928-8649

**Bureau of Patents, Trademarks,
& Technology Transfer**
3/F Trade and Industry Building
Senator Gil Puyat Avenue
Makati City
Tel/Fax: (632) 890-4901

**Bureau of Trade Regulation
& Consumer Protection**
3/F Trade and Industry Building
Senator Gil Puyat Avenue
Makati City
Tel/Fax: (632) 890-4901

**Centre for International Trade
Expositions & Missions**
International Trade
Centre Complex
Roxas Boulevard, Pasay City
Tel/Fax: (632) 831-2201,
Fax 832-3965

Central Bank of the Philippines
Mabini Street, Ermita
Manila
Tel/Fax: (632) 524-7011

**Department of Agrarian Reform
(DAR)**
Quezon Memorial Circle
Quezon City
Tel/Fax: (632) 928-7031

Department of Foreign Affairs (DFA)
2330 Roxas Boulevard
Manila
Tel/Fax: (632) 834-4444

Department of Health (DOH)
San Lazaro Compound
Santa Cruz, Manila
Tel/Fax: (632) 711-6290

Department of Justice (DOJ)
Maria Orosa Street corner
Padre Faura, Ermita, Manila
Tel/Fax: (632) 524-7409

Department of Labour and Employment (DOLE)
Muralla Street, Intramuros, Manila
Tel/Fax: (632) 527-3577, 527-2126

Department of Transportation & Communications (DOTC)
Philcomcen Building
Pasig City
Tel/Fax: (632) 631-8761, 631-8666, 632-0453

Department of National Defence (DND)
Camp Emilio Aguinaldo
Santolan Street, Quezon City
Tel/Fax: (632) 911-8944, 911-4452

Department of Science and Technology (DOST)
General Santos Avenue
Bicutan, Taguig
Tel/Fax: (632) 822-0961 to 67

Department of Trade and Industry (DTI)
Trade and Industry Building
Senator Gil Puyat Avenue
Makati City
Tel/Fax: (632) 890-4901

Environment Management Bureau
Visayas Avenue, Quezon City
Tel/Fax: (632) 928-0691

Export Assistance Network (Exponet)
6/F New Solid Building
Senator Gil Puyat Avenue
Makati City
Tel/Fax: (632) 818-8434

Philippine Export Processing Zone (PEZA)
4/F Legaspi Towers 300
Vito Cruz & Roxas Boulevard
Manila
Tel/Fax: (632) 521-0546, 521-0542

Garment & Textile Export Board (GTEB)
3-5/F New Solid Building
Senator Gil Puyat Avenue
Makati City
Tel/Fax: (632) 890-4648, 890-4699

**Housing and Land Use
Regulatory Board**
Elliptical Road
Quezon City
Tel/Fax: (632) 928-4561, 922-1912

**Land Transportation, Franchising
& Regulatory Board**
LTO Compound
East Avenue, Quezon City
Tel/Fax: (632) 921-2616, 921-2291

**Manila Electric
Company (Meralco)**
Meralco Lopez Building
Ortigas Avenue, Pasig City
Tel/Fax: (632) 631-2222, 631-5581
MEDICARE
8/F Philippine Heart Centre
Building
East Avenue, Diliman,
Quezon City
Tel/Fax: (632) 927-1272

Metro Manila Authority (MMA)
Orense Street corner EDSA
Guadalupe, Makati City
Tel/Fax: (632) 815-1722 to 24

**Metropolitan Waterworks
& Sewage System (MWSS)**
MWSS Complex, Katipunan Road
Balara, Quezon City
Tel/Fax: (632) 924-2074, 928-5650

**National Subcontractors
Exchange**
3/F Oppen Building
349 Senator Gil Puyat Avenue
Makati City
Tel/Fax: (632) 815-4584, 818-9111

**National Telecommunications
Commission (NTC)**
865 Vibal Building
EDSA corner Times Street
Quezon City
Tel/Fax: (632) 924-4042

Office of Energy Affairs (OEA)
PNOC Complex, Merit Road
Fort Bonifacio, Makati City
Tel/Fax: (632) 892-4619, 818-2416

Philippine Coconut Authority
M. Marcos Avenue, Quezon City
Tel/Fax: (632) 928-4501
**Philippine International Trading
Corporation (PITC)**
PITC Building, Tordesillas Street
Makati City
Tel/Fax: (632) 818-9810, 917-2314

Philippine Ports Authority (PPA)
Marsman Building, South Harbour
Port Area, Manila
Tel/Fax: (632) 527-8378

Philippine Shippers Council
5/F Trade and Industry Building
Senator Gil Puyat Avenue
Makati City
Tel/Fax: (632) 818-5705, 817-5451

**Product Development & Design
Centre of the Philippines**
CCP Complex
Roxas Boulevard, Manila
Tel/Fax: (632) 832-1112 to 19

Social Security System (SSS)
SSS Building
East Avenue, Diliman
Quezon City
Tel/Fax: (632) 921-2131, 921-0660

**Securities and
Exchange Commission (SEC)**
SEC Building
EDSA, Mandaluyong City
Tel/Fax: (632) 721-5035, 721-4057

Twelve Major Dailies for Advertising

Business Daily
Suite 212, 216–218
BF Condominium, Aduana Street
Intramuros, Manila
Tel: (632) 527-6701 to 08,
527-6761 to 64
Fax: (632) 527-3339, 527-3412

Business World
95 Balete Drive Extension
New Manila, Quezon City
Tel: (632) 721-9638, 721-1664
Fax: (632) 721-1664

Daily Inquirer
Chino Roces Corner Yague Street
Makati City
Tel: (632) 897-8808
Fax: (632) 897-4793, 897-4806

Evening Paper
37 Scout Limbaga, Quezon City
Tel: (632) 924-3571 to 72
Fax: (632) 924-3573 to 74

Malaya
575 Atlanta Street
Port Area, Manila
Tel: (632) 492-531, 482-209, 482-220
Fax (632) 530-1051, 530-1208

Manila Bulletin & Tempo
Muralla Corner Recoletos Street
Intramuros, Manila
Tel: (632) 527-8126, 527-8121
Fax: (632) 499-050

Manila Chronicle
371 Bonifacio Drive
Port Area, Manila
Tel: (632) 527-8101
Fax: (632) 527-0628, 527-0640

Manila Standard
Kamahalan Publishing Corp
Railroad and 21st Street
Port Area, Manila
Tel: (632) 527-8351, 407-790
Fax: (632) 467-558

Manila Times
Metro Media Times Corporation
30 EDSA corner Pioneer Street
Mandaluyong City
Tel: (632) 631-8971, 631-8985
Fax: (632) 631-7788

Today
Independent Daily News, Inc.
Macrisma Building, 1666 EDSA corner
Escuela Street, Makati City
Tel: (632) 894-0644, 818-1333
Fax: (632) 844-3093

Philippine Star
13th and Railroad Streets
Port Area, Manila
Tel: (632) 527-7905, 405-431
Fax: (632) 404-985

Times Journal, Tonite, People
Journal Building
Railroad & 19th/20th Streets
Port Area, Manila
Tel: (632) 527-8421, 5278440
Fax: (632) 527-4672

Important Tourist Information Centres

Department of Tourism
DOT Building, Teodoro
Valencia Circle
Rizal Park, Ermita, Manila
Tel: (632) 599-031,
Fax: (632) 524-2103

Department of Tourism
Ninoy Aquino
International Airport
Pasay City, Metro Manila
Tel: (632) 832-2964,
(632) 832-1165

Philippine Convention and Visitors Corporation
4th Floor, Units 5, 7,10-17
Legaspi Towers 300
Roxas Boulevard, Manila
Tel: (632) 575-031,
Fax: (632) 521-6165

24-Hour Tourist Assistance Hotlines
Tel: (632) 501-728, (632) 501-660

6-Days-A-Week Tourist Service
Department of Tourism Gallery
Tel: 501-703, 599-031 local 146

Ninoy Aquino International Airport (NAIA)
Tel: (632) 828-4791, 828-1511

Cebu City:
Tel: 91-503, 96-518

Davao City:
Tel: (82) 64-688, (82) 71-534

Overseas Tourist Information Offices

Australia
Philippine Department of Tourism
Highmount House, Level 6
122 Castlereagh Street,
Sydney N.S.W. 2000,
Australia
Tel: (2) 267-2695, (2) 267-2756
Fax: (02) 283-1862

Germany
Philippine Department of Tourism
Kaiser Strasse 15, 60311 Frankfurt
Main 1, Frankfurt, Germany
Tel: (069) 20893, (069) 20894
Fax: (069) 285-127

Hong Kong
6/F United Centre
95 Queensway, Hong Kong
Tel: (852) 866-7665,
(852) 866-6471
Fax: (852) 866-6521

Japan
Embassy of the Philippines 11-24
Nampeidai Machi, Shibuya-Ku
Tokyo, Japan
Tel: (03) 3464-3630
Fax: (03) 3464-3690

Korea
1107, Renaissance Building
1598-3 Socho-Dong, Socho-Ku
Seoul, Korea (137-070)
Fax: 82 (02) 525-1708

Singapore
Philippine Tourism Office
400 Orchard Road
#06-24 Orchard Towers
Singapore 238875
Tel: (65) 738-7165,
Fax: (65) 738-2604
E-mail:
philtours_sin@pacific.net.sg

Taiwan
Manila Economic and
Cultural Office
4/F Metrobank Plaza
107 Chung Hsioo E. Road
Section 4, Taipei,
Taiwan, ROC
Tel: 741-5994
Fax: 866 (2) 778-4969

United Kingdom
Philippine Department of Tourism
17 Albemarle Street
London WIX 4LX
United Kingdom
Tel: (0171) 499-5443
Fax: (0171) 499-5772

United States of America
Philippine Consulate General
3660 Wilshire Boulevard
900 Suite 825
Los Angeles, CA 90010, USA
Tel: (213) 487-4527
Fax: (213) 386-4063

Philippine Center
556 Fifth Avenue
New York, NY 10036, USA
Tel: (212) 575-7915
Fax: (212) 302-6759

Web Sites

Here are some useful Philippine websites to visit:
www.yahoo.com/Regional/Countries/Philippines/
Government: www.philippines.gov.ph/
Trade and Investments: www.dti.gov.ph/
News from Major Publications: www.philnews.com/
Travel Information, Airports, Airlines, Flying:
www.asia-online.com/travel/essen/ph.html
Online Accommodation Information:
www.traveler.net/htio/hotels/asia/philipp.html
American Embassy in the Philippines:
www.mozcom.com/USIS/Home.html
Travel Advisory Sheet: travel.state.gov/philippines.html
General Information and Maps:
www.teachersoft.com/Library/ref/atlas/asia/rp.htm
Law Firms: hg.org/firms-philippines.html

APPENDIX C

References

Office of the President. *Handbook on Doing Business in the Philippines.* Manila: Coordinating Council of the Philippine Assistance Programme, 1995.

Tan Teck Meng, Low Aik Meng, John J. Williams and Luis Ma. R. Calingo. *Business Opportunities in the Philippines.* Singapore: Prentice Hall, 1996.

Abella, Carmencita T. "Socio-Cultural Factors Influencing Firm-Level Productivity in the Philippines" in *Easternisation: Socio-Cultural Impact on Productivity.* ed. Kwang-Kuo Hwang. Tokyo: Asian Productivity Organisation, 1995, pp 234-267.

Andres, Tomas. *Understanding Filipino Values: A Management Approach.* Quezon City, Philippines: New Day Publishers, 1981.

Church, A. Timothy. *Filipino Personality: A Review of Research and Writings.* Manila: De La Salle University Press, 1986.

"Corruption in Asia in 1987" *Asian Intelligence,* Issue #482, 26 March 1997.

Dolan, Ronald E. *Philippines: A Country Study.* Washington, D.C.: Library of Congress, Federal Research Division, 1991.

Dunung, Sanjyot P. *Doing Business in Asia: The Complete Guide.* New York: Lexington Books, 1995.

Economist Intelligence Unit. *Investing, Licensing & Trading: Philippines.* London: Economist Intelligence Unit Limited, 1997.

Grimes, Barbara F., ed. *Ethnologue.* 13th ed. Dallas: Summer Institute of Logistics, 1996.

Hofstede, Geert. *Cultures and Organisations: Software of the Mind.* New York: McGraw-Hill, 1997.

Likert, Rensis. *The Human Organisation.* New York: McGraw-Hill, 1967.

Nolan, James L., et al. *Philippines Business: The Portable Encyclopedia for Doing Business in the Philippines.* San Rafael, California: Word Trade Press, 1996.

Roces, Alfredo and Grace. *Culture Shock! Philippines.* Singapore: Times Books International, 1985.

United Nations Development Programme. *UNDP Human Development Report 1997.* New York: Oxford University Press, 1997.

Notes

Chapter 4

1. As of 20 October 1997, the currency exchange rate was US$1 = PHP34.45. All dollar figures in this chapter are in US dollars.

2. A Republic Act (RA) is a public law enacted by the Philippine Government in the period 1946–1972 and 1986–present. In contrast, a Presidential Decree (PD) is a public law promulgated by President Ferdinand E. Marcos during his authoritarian regime (1972–1986). Many of these PDs were subsequently recognised by the Aquino and Ramos administrations and are still in effect.

3. Monetary authorities have given unibanks two years to raise the minimum capitalisation from PHP2.5 billion to PHP4.5 billion (about US$131 million) beginning in 1997.

4. Under a 1995 order by President Ramos, government offices are required to render extended hours of service from 7.00 a.m. to 7.00 p.m. Government employees may now choose to work either from 7.00 a.m. to 4.00 p.m. or from 10.00 a.m. to 7.00 p.m.; thus the 40-hour week remains.

5. The US dollar equivalents of the wage rates in this paragraph are based on the US$1 = PHP26.37 exchange rate prevailing prior to the July-August 1997 peso devaluation.

6. The government-run PAG-IBIG [Tagalog for "love"] Fund provides social security benefits to member-employees. Both employees and employers contribute to the PAG-IBIG Fund.

Chapter 6

1. Andres, Tomas D. *Understanding Filipino Values: A Management Approach* Quezon City, Philippines: New Day Publishers, 1981, pp 78–79.

2. In terms of the leadership literature, the Filipino's paternalistic leadership style is equivalent to Likert's System 2 (Benevolent Autocrat). See Rensis Likert's *The Human Organisation*. New York: McGraw-Hill, 1967.

3. "Corruption in Asia in 1997", *Asian Intelligence*. Issue #482, March 26, 1997.

4. United Nations Development Programme. *UNDP Human Development Report 1997*. New York: Oxford University Press, 1997, p 41.

Chapter 7

1. Abella, Carmencita T. "Socio-Cultural Factors Influencing Firm-Level Productivity in the Philippines" in *Easternisation: Socio-Cultural Impact on Productivity.* ed. Kwang-Kuo Hwang. Tokyo: Asian Productivity Organisation, 1995, pp 234–267.
2. Hofstede, Geert. *Cultures and Organisations: Software of the Mind.* New York: McGraw-Hill, 1997, p 26.
3. Church, A. Timothy. *Filipino Personality: A Review of Research and Writings.* Manila: De La Salle University Press, 1986, pp 10–12.
4. Barbara F. Grimes, Ed., *Ethnologue*, 13th ed. Dallas: Summer Institute of Linguistics, 1996.

About the Authors

JOAQUIN L. GONZALEZ, PhD is a lecturer of Public Policy and Administration at the Department of Political Science, National University of Singapore (NUS). Dr. Gonzalez is concurrently the Regional Research Coordinator of the Canada-ASEAN Governance Innovations Network (CAGIN). Prior to joining NUS, he was attached to the Policy Research and Operations Policy Departments of the World Bank in Washington, DC (USA). Dr. Gonzalez also worked for the Philippine Presidential Commission on Government Reorganisation (PCGR) and the Congress of the Philippines.

LUIS R. CALINGO, PhD is a professor of International Management at the Monterey Institute of International Studies. He has served as a consultant to numerous organisations in the United States and Southeast Asia in the areas of strategic management, total quality management and cultural differences management. Professor Calingo has previously taught at California State University (Fresno), Nanyang Business School (Singapore) and the University of the Philippines.

Index

accommodation, 178

agrarian reform, 42, 57, 58, 89, 110

agriculture, 12, 16, 22, 36, 41, 44, 56, 61, 65, 89, 93, 98, 99, 110, 117, 124, 125, 132, 165

agro-industrial, 20, 61, 110, 111, 124, 127, 136

airport, 118, 122, 129, 136, 137, 141, 179, 183

Aquino, Corazon C., 17, 45, 47, 48, 50, 56, 154, 167–169, 199

Armed Forces of the Philippines (AFP), 25, 45, 62, 63, 68

ASEAN Free Trade Area (AFTA), 28, 105

Asia-Europe Meeting (ASEM), 28, 31, 32

Asia-Pacific Economic Cooperation (APEC), 24, 28–31, 33, 83, 105

Asian Development Bank (ADB), 28, 30–32, 35, 85, 88, 89, 120

Association of Southeast Asian Nations (ASEAN), 28, 29, 32, 47, 83, 108, 133

Australia, 13, 27, 29, 34, 118, 133, 178

Bangko Sentral ng Pilipinas (BSP), 74, 76, 79, 88–91, 95

Bangkok, 115, 178

Bank Liberalisation Law, 86

banking, 17, 49, 65, 84–89, 91, 117, 164, 180

barangays, 36, 60, 61, 70, 136, 164

barong Tagalog, 152, 153, 184

bilateral ties, 23, 26, 27, 45

Board of Investments (BOI), 14, 73, 78–82, 102, 103, 106, 143, 144

Brunei Darussalam, 28, 29, 34, 115, 133

Buddhists, 170, 171

Build-operate-and-transfer (BOT), 49, 50, 58, 121, 123

building permits, 78, 82

Bureau of Customs (BOC), 81, 94, 103

Bureau of Export Trade Promotion (BETP), 56

business hours, 151, 180

Cebu, 51, 130, 140, 168, 171, 179, 182

China, 13, 29, 34, 37, 38, 40, 41, 66, 182

Christianity, 69, 158, 170, 171

Civil Service Commission (CSC), 59, 60

Clark Development Corporation, 115–117, 119

Clark Special Economic Zone (CSEZ), 80, 112–119

Clean Report of Findings (CRF), 84, 104

coconuts, 36, 105, 137

collective bargaining, 96, 99, 101

colleges, 163, 164, 169

Common Effective Preferential Tariff
    (CEPT), 29, 83
communications, 24, 61, 92, 93, 138,
    156, 164, 169, 180
Constitutions, 44, 46, 48, 57, 59, 63,
    91, 110, 155
construction, 25, 120, 167
corruption, 48, 64, 104, 148,
    150, 151, 199
countryside, 18, 49, 62, 98, 165
credit, 42, 61, 84, 88
crime, 18, 100
cronies and technocrats, 48, 63, 67,
    68
culture, 20, 23, 36, 44, 65, 156, 172
currencies, 51, 89–91, 180
current-account transactions, 90
customs, 35, 53, 79, 81, 83, 84,
    102–105, 181

defence, 16, 62, 77, 94, 118
Department of Environment and
    Natural Resources (DENR), 77,
    81, 94, 106, 143
Department of Finance, 76, 79
Department of Labour and Employ-
    ment (DOLE), 76, 94, 97, 99,
    100
Department of Tourism, 38, 81, 94,
    138, 143, 144, 182, 193
Department of Trade and Industry
    (DTI), 20, 53, 79
deregularisation, 51
dialects, 66, 168
District Agro-Industrial Centres
    (DAICs), 129
duty-free, 181, 182

education, 16, 17, 22, 24, 41,
    61, 69, 91, 156, 163, 169,
    171–173
elections, 54, 60, 70, 71
electricity, 78, 115, 125, 167
electronic sector, 25, 26
encomiendas, 39
English, 25, 72, 95, 117, 157, 163
    168, 170–172, 177, 178
environment, 25, 61, 69, 72, 77, 94,
    105–107, 137
ethnic groups, 65, 125, 156
Europe, 13, 28, 31, 36, 41,
    66, 133, 134, 145, 162
exchange controls, 84, 89
Executive Branch, 46, 54, 56, 58
Export Assistance Network
    (Exponet), 56

financial institutions, 85, 89
foreign banks,
    49, 75, 86, 87, 89, 91
foreign corporations, 91, 92, 110
Foreign Investments Act, 49, 58, 77,
    79

gold, 38, 40, 90, 129, 134
government agencies, 53, 60, 79,
    80, 121
Gross Domestic Product, 16, 19
Gross National Product, 13, 19, 50,
    163
growth rate, 48, 50

healthcare, 19, 61, 77, 78, 94
Hong Kong, 13, 16, 18, 24, 27, 29,
    34, 90, 115, 163, 177, 183

hotels, 118, 131, 164, 179
housing, 58, 119
human resource, 34, 72, 119

immigration, 79, 102, 103
Implementing Rules and Regulations
    (IRR), 106, 107
imports, 16, 49, 79, 82, 83, 91, 93,
    103–105
incentives, 23, 60, 68, 79, 80, 112,
    118, 120, 124, 127, 135
India, 37, 38, 41, 66, 156
indigenous communities, 57, 107
Indonesia, 28, 29, 34, 104, 133, 156
inflation, 14, 16, 50
infrastructure, 16, 42, 49, 50, 61, 85,
    98, 106, 112, 114, 118–120,
    122, 124, 129, 132, 134, 138
insurance, 81, 85, 89, 91, 163
intellectual property, 35, 72, 107,
    108
interest rates, 14, 17, 51, 88
International Monetary Fund, 35
Investors' Lease Act, 110
investments, 12, 14, 16, 17, 20,
    22–24, 29, 30, 31, 36, 48, 50,
    51, 57, 61, 72, 77, 79, 80, 81,
    84, 85, 87, 89, 102, 107, 108,
    112, 113, 117–120, 124–144,
    182

Japan, 13, 16, 23, 26, 29, 34, 38,
    41, 43, 44, 47, 48, 75, 82,
    85, 118, 134, 149, 172, 177,
    178
joint ventures, 32, 72, 74, 118, 121
judicial branch, 46, 59

kinship, 158–162, 165

labour, 22, 58, 59, 69, 79, 93–102,
    166
land reform, 18, 69
languages, 65, 66, 156, 168–170,
    183
legislative branch, 54, 57
Letters of Credit (L/Cs), 81, 91, 104
liberalisation, 47, 72, 84, 105
licensing, 49, 72, 73
literacy, 19, 22, 95, 172
Local Government Code, 49, 60
Local Government Unit (LGU), 23,
    49, 60, 61, 82, 121–123

Makati, 164, 181
Malacanang Palace, 54, 183
Malaysia, 28, 29, 34, 118, 177
Manila, 12, 29, 39, 40, 43, 51 54, 98,
    109, 114, 124, 126, 141, 160
    162–164, 168, 173, 177–179,
    181–183
Manila Action Plan for APEC
    (MAPA 96), 29, 33
Manila Electric Company
    (MERALCO), 78, 127, 147
manufacturing, 16, 27, 72, 73, 98,
    112, 117, 124, 126
Marcos, Ferdinand E., 17, 45–48, 54,
    63, 64, 67, 68, 71, 167, 199
media, 53, 145, 164, 168, 169
mestizos, 40–44, 65, 66
Metro Manila, 12, 18, 57, 66, 67, 69,
    78, 98, 115, 124, 126, 138, 144
    152, 163, 164, 166–168, 172,
    180, 183
military, 25, 45, 53, 62, 68, 113

Mindanao, 32, 36, 131–137, 168,
    182
multinational corporations, 74, 75,
    95, 101, 144
municipalities, 53, 60, 61, 74, 103,
    107, 183

Newly Industrialising Country
    (NIC), 20, 47, 117
Ninoy Aquino International Airport
    (NAIAI), 127, 179

Official Development Assistance
    (ODA), 26, 27
Omnibus Investments Code of 1987,
    78, 91
One-Stop Action Centre (OSAC),
    79, 102, 144, 185
overseas Filipinos, 12, 17, 57, 95,
    182

Pacific Basin Economic Council
    (PBEC), 28, 34
Pacific Economic Cooperation
    Council (PECC), 28, 33
PAG-IBIG Fund, 99, 199
Pandanan Wreck, 15, 38
pearl, 38, 40
"Pearl of the Orient", 11, 38
"people power", 47, 48, 69
Philippine Airlines, 51, 65, 181, 183
Philippine Export Zone Authority
    (PEZA), 78–80, 92, 103
Pilipino, 168, 169, 171, 177, 183
Political and Economic Risk
    Consultancy (PERC), 18, 151
population, 19, 163, 177

postal services, 81, 179, 180
poverty, 18, 19, 48, 165, 166
pre-shipment inspection, 103, 104
Presidential Decree, 58, 59, 199
privatisation, 50, 51, 56, 108
Protestants, 69, 170, 171
punctuality, 151, 152

quasi-banks, 87
Quezon, 109, 127

Ramos, Fidel V., 19, 20, 30, 32, 45,
    47, 48, 50, 51, 56, 58, 106,
    107, 167, 168, 199
Regional Growth Centres, 22, 23
religion, 69, 147, 156, 158, 170,
    171
remittances, 17, 78–80, 91, 92, 95,
    137
road networks, 118, 126, 131
Roman Catholics, 69, 70, 142,
    145, 155, 170, 173, 177
rural areas, 22, 154, 164, 165, 172

San Miguel, 13, 65, 147
Securities and Exchange Commission
    (SEC), 72–76, 78–81, 92
SGS Inspection Services, 84, 103–
    105
shipping, 12, 49, 65, 117
Singapore, 16, 27–29, 34, 115, 118,
    133, 151, 177, 183
single proprietorship, 72, 79
small and medium enterprises, 20,
    22, 33, 49, 77, 93, 130
Social Security System, 76, 78, 89
social welfare, 16, 61

South Korea, 34
Southeast Asia, 14, 20, 25–28, 32,
        37, 38, 62, 85, 108, 154, 163,
        172, 177
Spain, 13, 17, 38, 39, 38–42, 59, 65,
        140, 142, 155, 156, 162, 172,
        183
Subic Bay Freeport, 62, 80, 112–120

Tagalog, 168–170, 175, 176
Taiwan, 16, 27, 29, 34, 118, 163,
        177, 182
tariffs, 29, 49, 83, 84, 103–105, 124
taxation, 13, 49, 51, 53, 60, 61, 72,
        92, 93, 103, 112, 117, 124, 137
telecommunications, 12, 25, 34, 49,
    ·   61, 81, 94, 118, 120, 124,
        125, 129, 132, 134
Thailand, 27–29, 32, 33, 177
thrift banks, 85, 89
tourism, 20, 34, 56, 61, 81,
        94, 102, 110, 112, 117,
        119, 124, 135, 137–141, 184
trade unions, 101
trademarks, 73, 94, 108
transportation, 112, 120, 144, 166
Treasury bills, 17, 87, 88

unibanks, 85–87, 199
United Kingdom, 13, 27, 117
United Nations, 35, 199
United States, 13, 23–26, 29, 30,
        34, 38, 41–45, 47, 54,
        62, 63, 66, 68, 85, 108, 113,
        114, 118, 134, 146, 163, 183
urbanisation, 19, 163
utilities, 16, 27, 77, 78, 112, 119,
        120, 124

Value Added Tax, 105
visas, 74, 102, 103, 182

Wage Rationalisation Act, 58, 97, 98
wages, 97, 98
women, 69, 96, 145, 147, 152,
        154, 155
World Bank, 35, 85, 88, 89, 119, 120
World Trade Organisation (WTO),
        32, 35, 105